Kamloops British Columbia Canada Book 2 in Colour Photos, Saving Our History One Photo at a Time

Photography
by Barbara Raué
©2019

Series Name:
Cruising Canada

Book 16: Kamloops Book 2

Cover photo: 245 St. Paul Street, Page 5

© 2019 by Barbara Raue - All the photos in this book have been taken with my cameras. I own the rights to them.

Series Name: Cruising Canada
Saving Our History One Photo at a Time
in colour photos

Book 1-9: Winnipeg Manitoba
Book 10: Osoyoos, B.C.
Book 11: Vernon, Salmon Arm
Book 12: Kelowna
Book 13: Penticton
Book 14: Hope
Book 15-17: Kamloops

Table of Contents

St. Paul Street   Page 4

Battle Street   Page 37

Kamloops is a city in south central British Columbia in Canada, located at the confluence of the two branches of the Thompson River near Kamloops Lake.

The first European explorer, David Stuart, arrived in 1811; he was sent out from Fort Astoria, a Pacific Fur Company post; he spent a winter there with the Secwepemc people. He and Alexander Ross established a post there in May 1812, "Fort Cumcloups".

The rival North West Company established another post, Fort Shuswap, nearby in the same year. The two operations were merged in 1813 when the North West Company officials in the region bought out the operations of the Pacific Fur Company. After the North West Company's forced merger with the Hudson's Bay Company in 1821, the post became known commonly as Thompson's River Post, or Fort Thompson, which over time became known as Fort Kamloops.

After the fur trade arrived in 1812, Kamloops became the crossroads for horse-drawn pack trains. In the years that followed, Kamloops' reputation as a bristling locality for trade and commerce was greatly broadened by the gold rush of the 1850s, among other things. Following the arrival of the first permanent ranchers was the railway which came through in 1893; Kamloops continued to be the resting stop for the weary travelers. Kamloops has continued to grow since then with cattle ranching, forestry and mining.

The gold rush of the 1860s and the construction of the Canadian Pacific Railway, which reached Kamloops from the West in 1883, brought further growth.

Pulp, plywood, veneer, cement, and a copper mine are industries in Kamloops. The Royal Inland Hospital is the city's largest employer. Thompson River University serves a student body of 10,000.

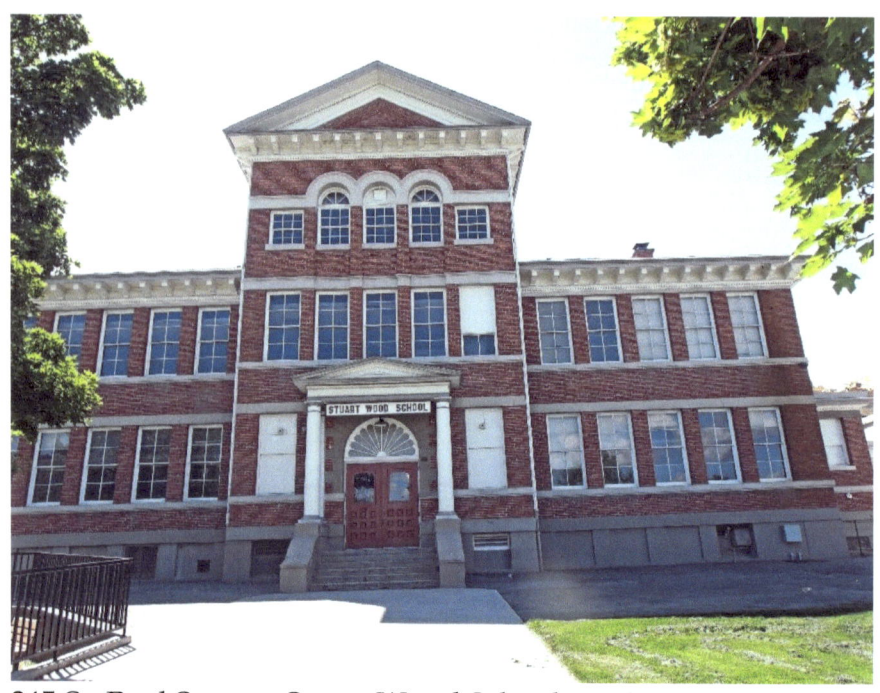

245 St. Paul Street – Stuart Wood School – 1907 – It is a three-story school, with a full-height basement, with a symmetrical façade in the Neo-Classical style. It is clad in red brick, has a broad hip roof, front and rear gabled projections, and parged stringcourses. The architecture conveys a sense of permanence and order and demonstrates the Romanesque Revival style in its massive masonry construction and round-arched windows. There are arched transoms above the three central windows on the third floor. The Classical Revival is evident in the pedimented portico, classical columns, and arched fanlight window above the central entrance. The large sash windows were characteristic of contemporary school design, arranged to take advantage of natural light and ventilation. It has been in continuous use as a school for over a century.

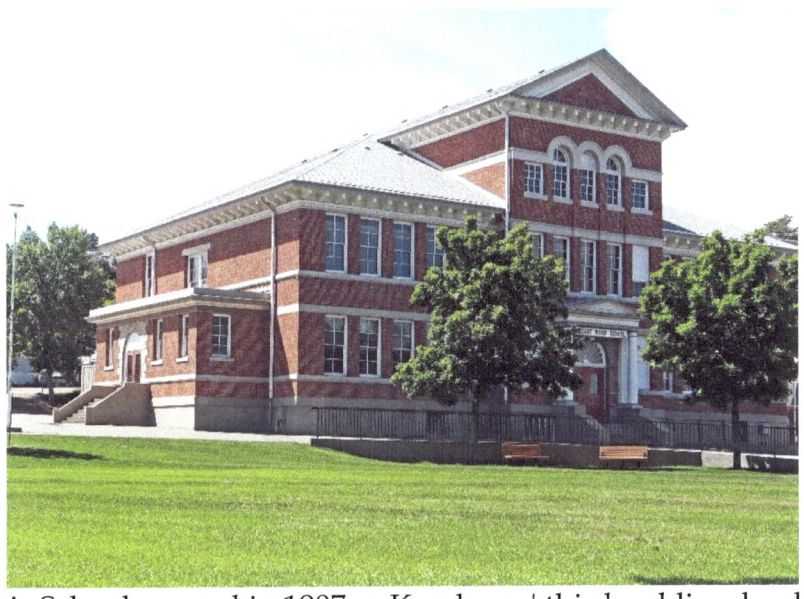

This School opened in 1907 as Kamloops' third public school. In 1922, the city named the building Stuart Wood School in honor of Kamloops' first public school teacher, E. Stuart Wood, who served the community from 1886 to 1910. This magnificent brick building was designed in a neoclassical style to underline the important place education holds in society. The columns on the front north entrance distinguish the school as a 'temple of knowledge'.

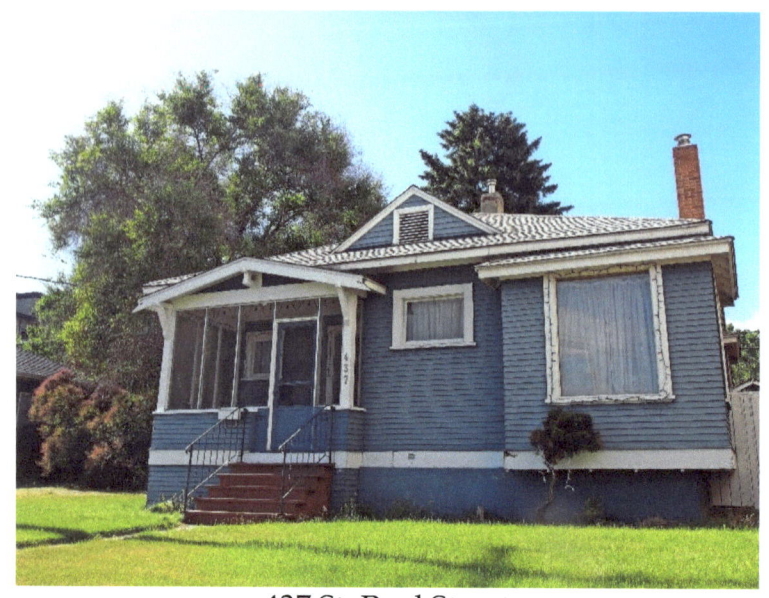

437 St. Paul Street

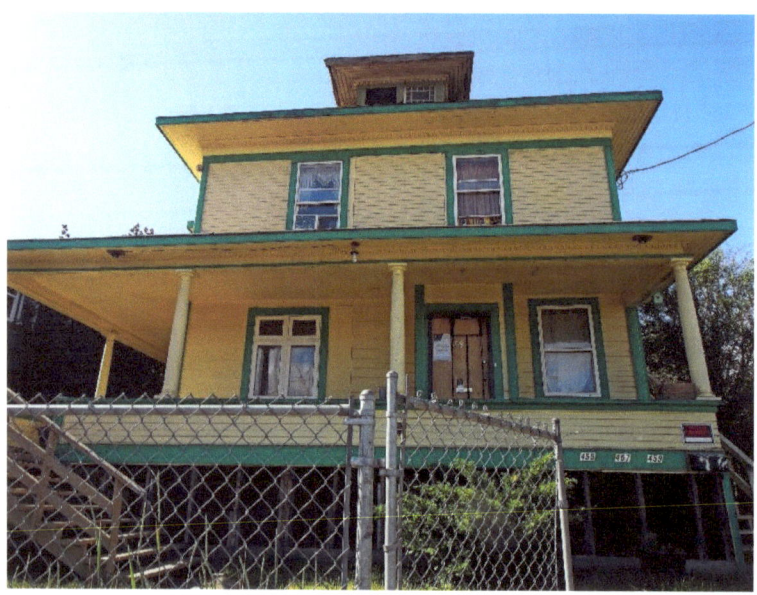

455-459 St. Paul Street - dormer

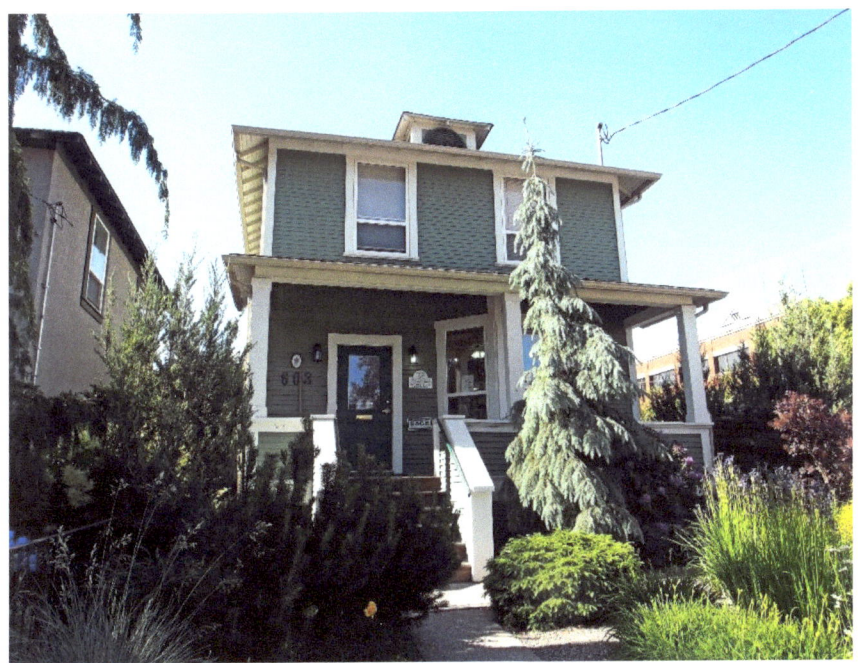

603 St. Paul Street - This Classic Box style house built in 1911 was popular at the beginning of the twentieth century. There are numerous examples throughout the older sections of the city. Typically, it has clapboard siding, v board soffits and wood rafter fascia. Because this house has been used for commercial use many of the original windows and doors have been replaced to meet modern building codes.

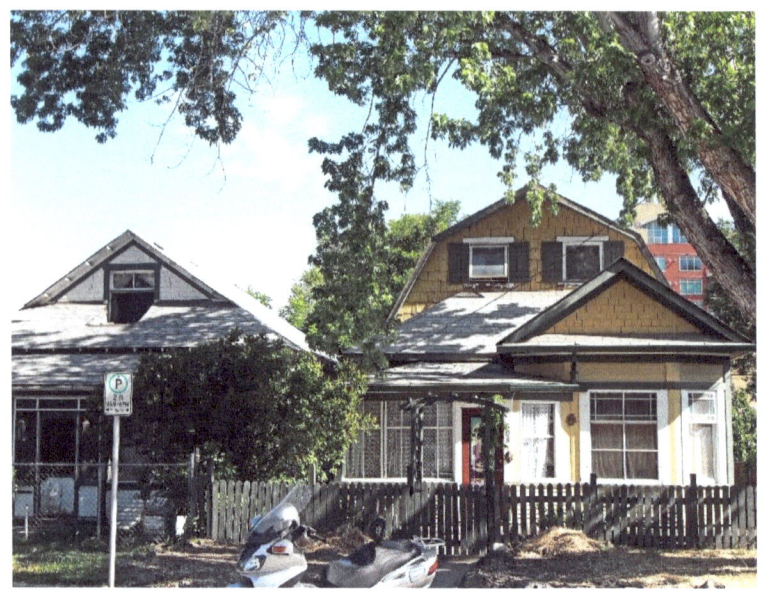

608 St. Paul Street – gambrel roof

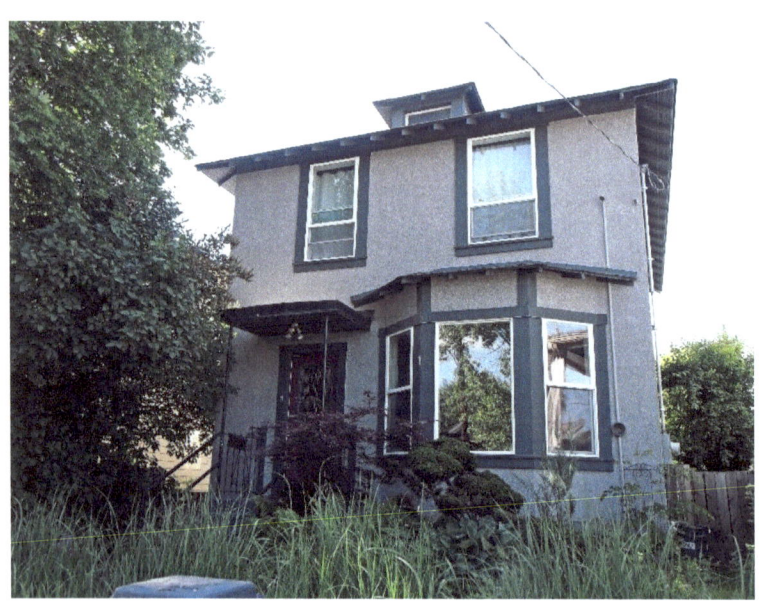

609 St. Paul Street – Classic Box style house - dormer, bay window

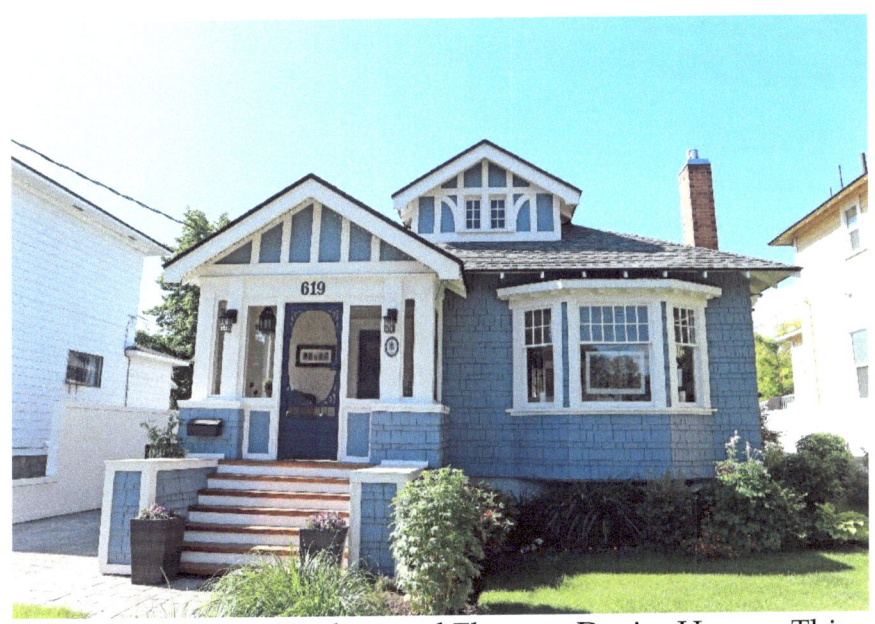

619 St. Paul Street - Herbert and Florence Davies House - This home is a classic example of the Craftsman style house in Kamloops. It was built in 1924 during one of the greatest economic boom times in Kamloops' history. The first owners were Herbert and Florence Davies. Herbert Davies was a contractor, so it is very likely he built this house himself. As a contractor, Herbert was well-known for his work on the city hall addition in 1913, as well as houses at Seventh Avenue and Dominion.

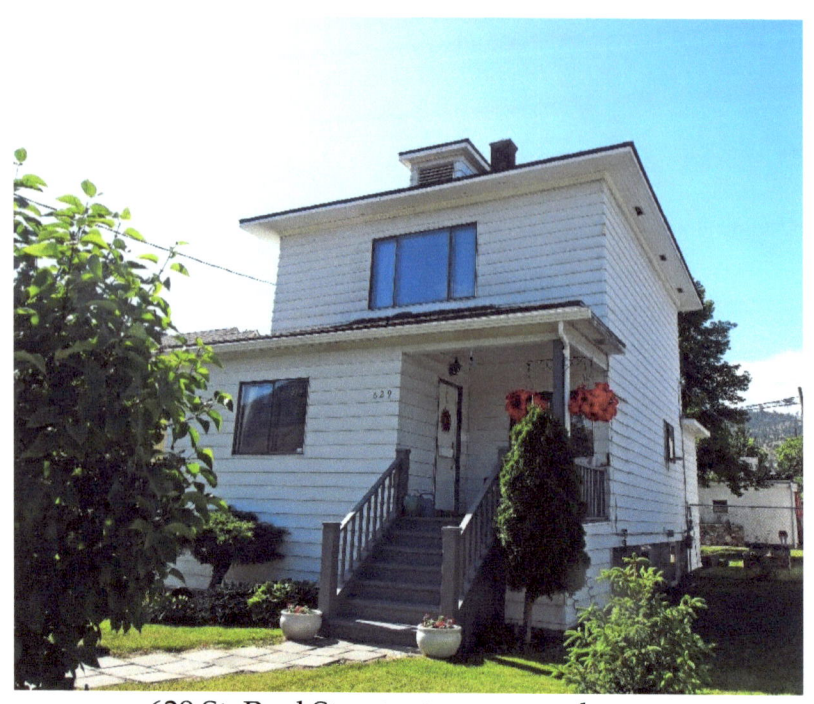

629 St. Paul Street – two-story, dormer

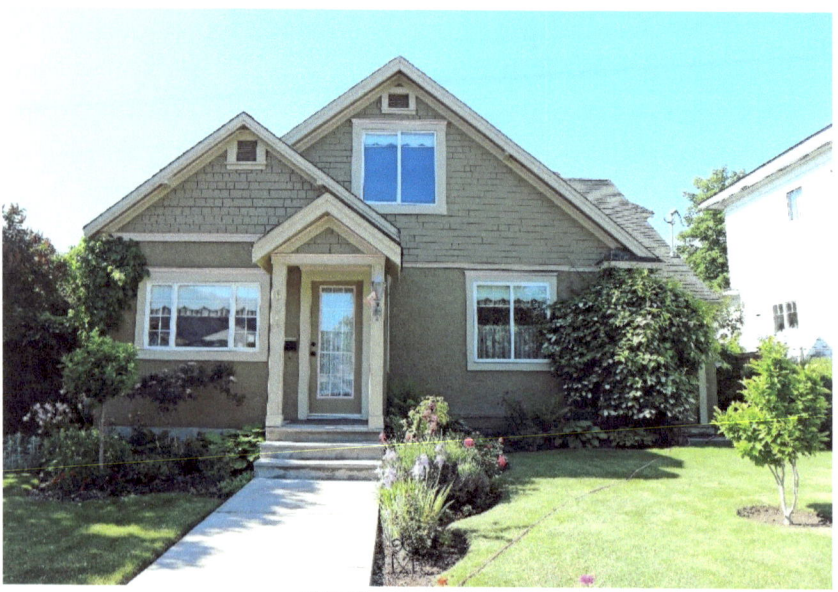

635 St. Paul Street

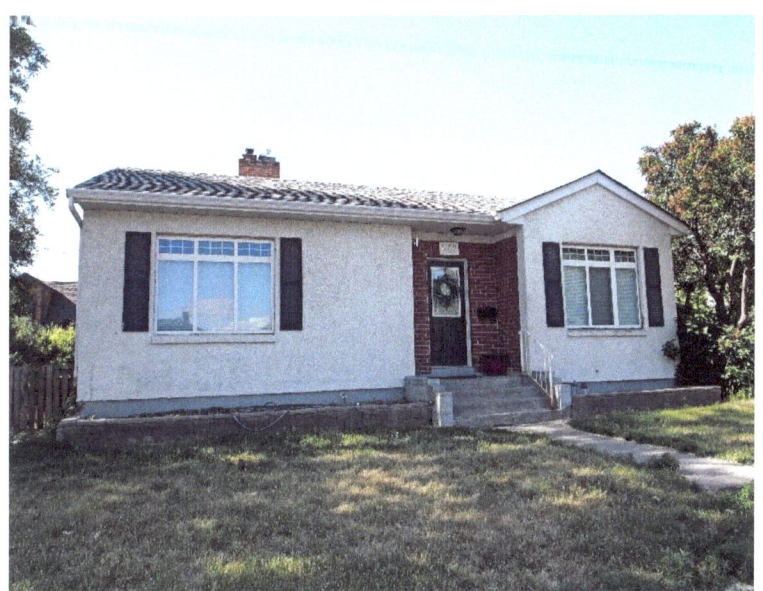

647 St. Paul Street

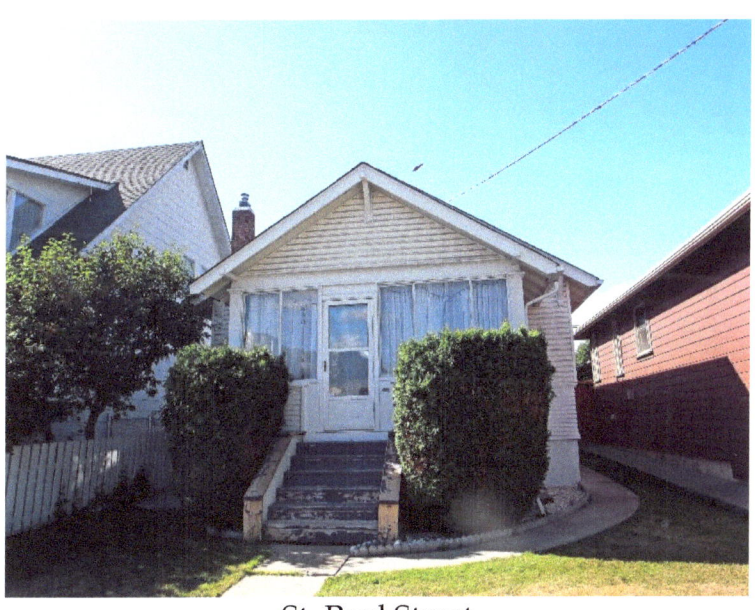

St. Paul Street

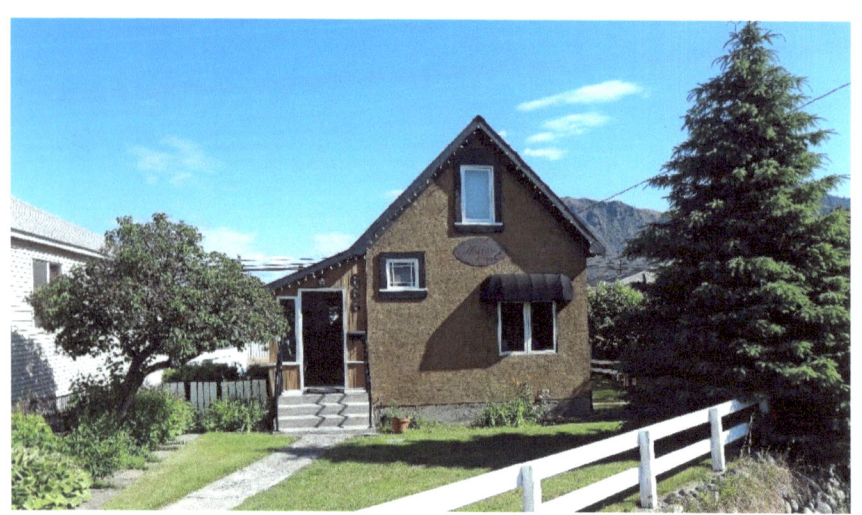

666 St. Paul Street

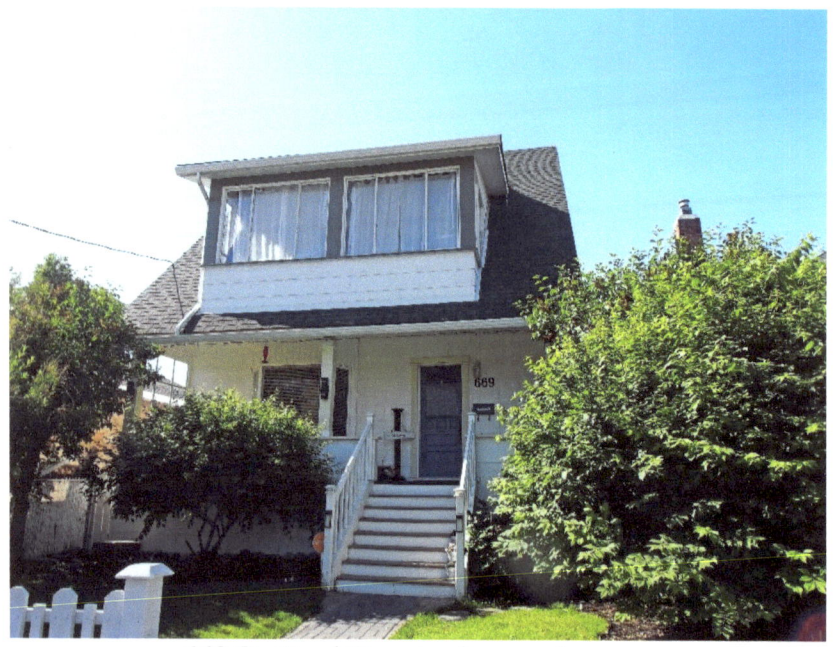

669 St. Paul Street – larger dormer

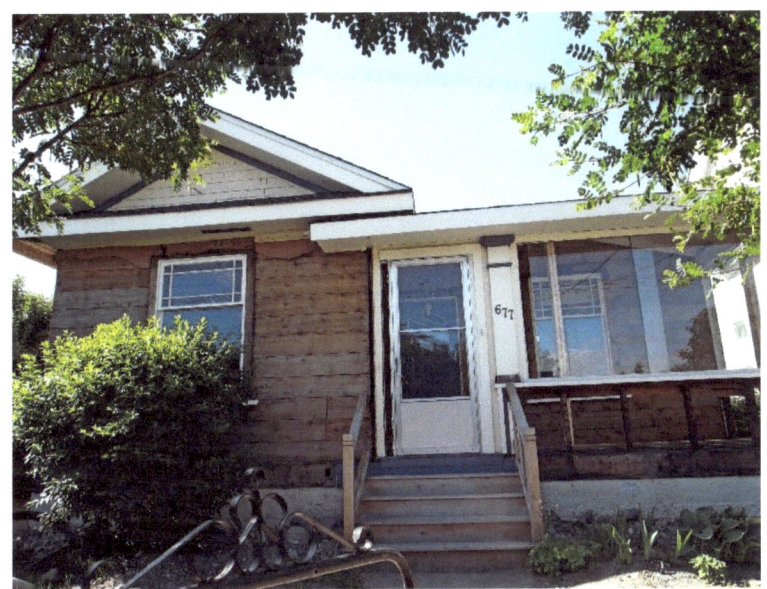

677 St. Paul Street

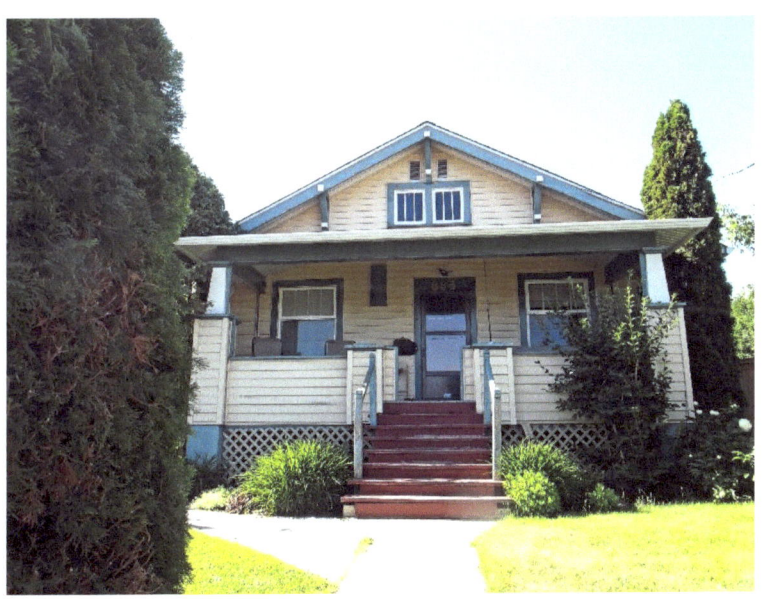

683 St. Paul Street

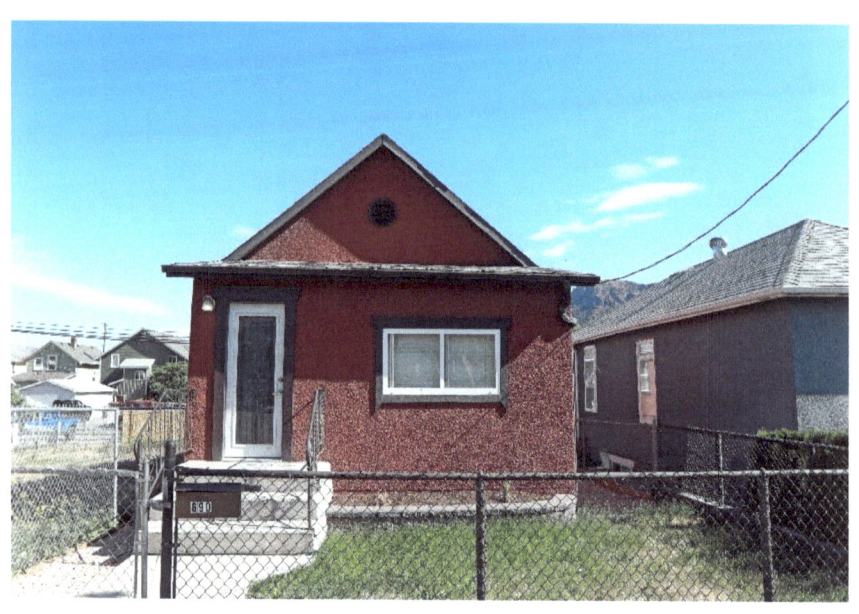

690 St. Paul Street – circular window in gable

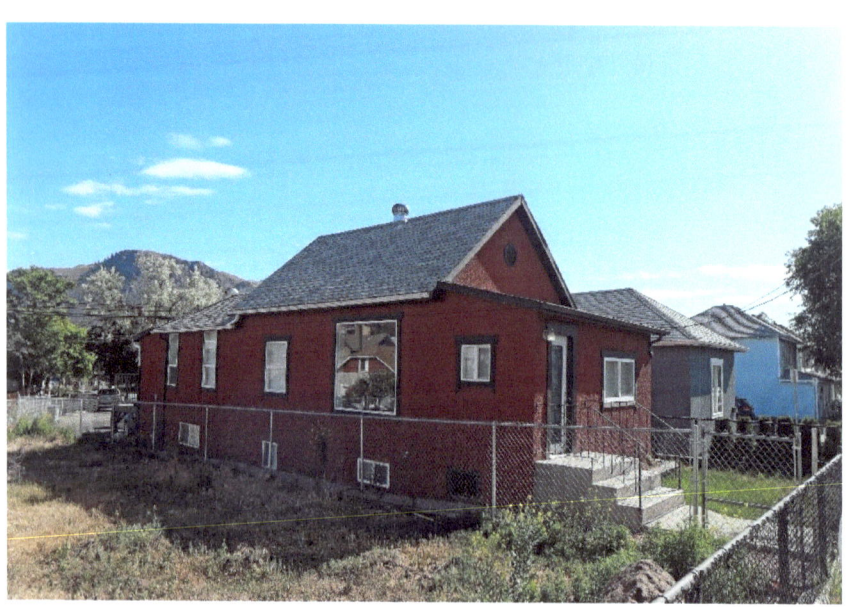

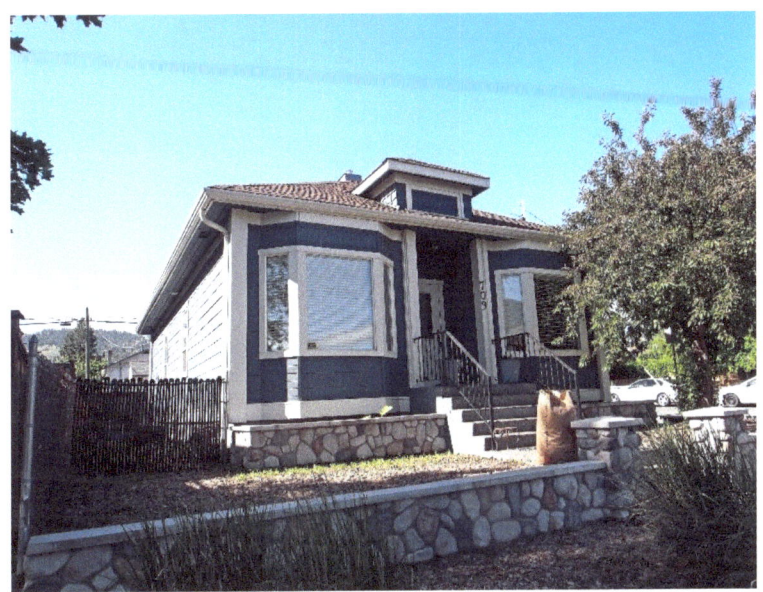

703 St. Paul Street – dormer, bay windows

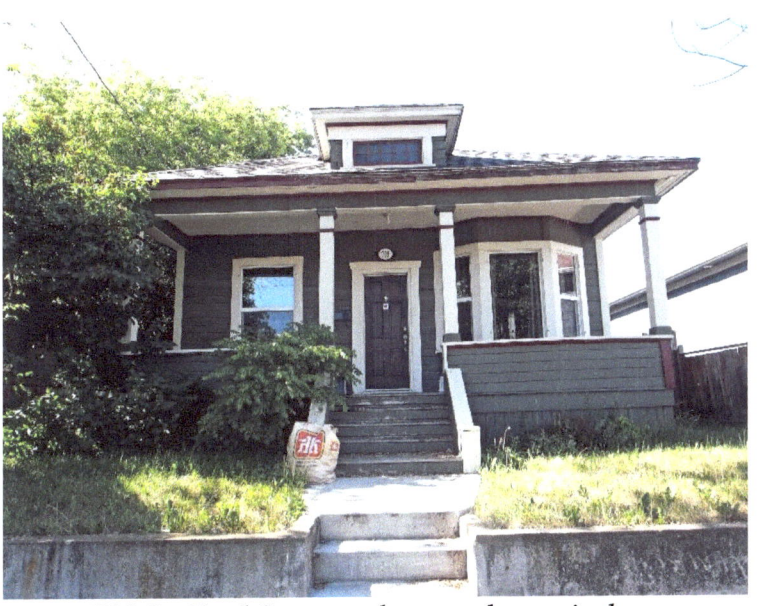

709 St. Paul Street – dormer, bay window

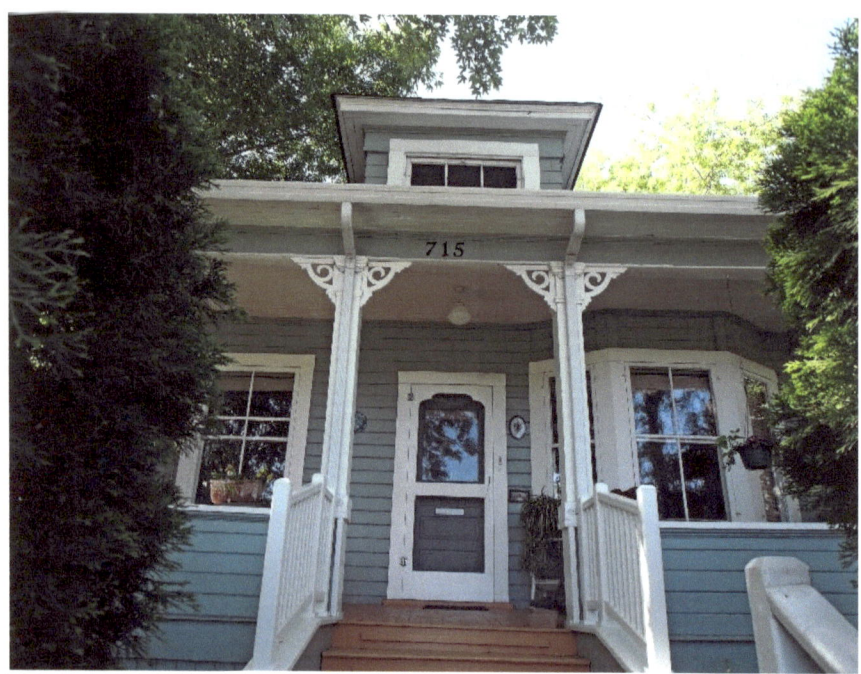

715 St. Paul Street - This is one of a dozen identical houses built in this block by an English contractor between 1913 - 1923. Craftsman in style this house was built in 1913. It has v board soffits, wood rafter fascia, broad weather board siding and wood frame widows. The verandah has four square pillars that is common to this style and the front door is original.

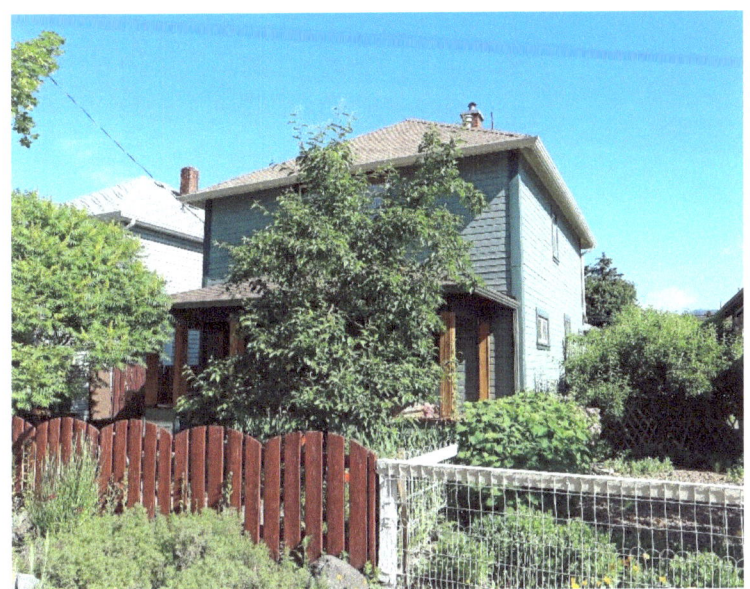

714 St. Paul Street

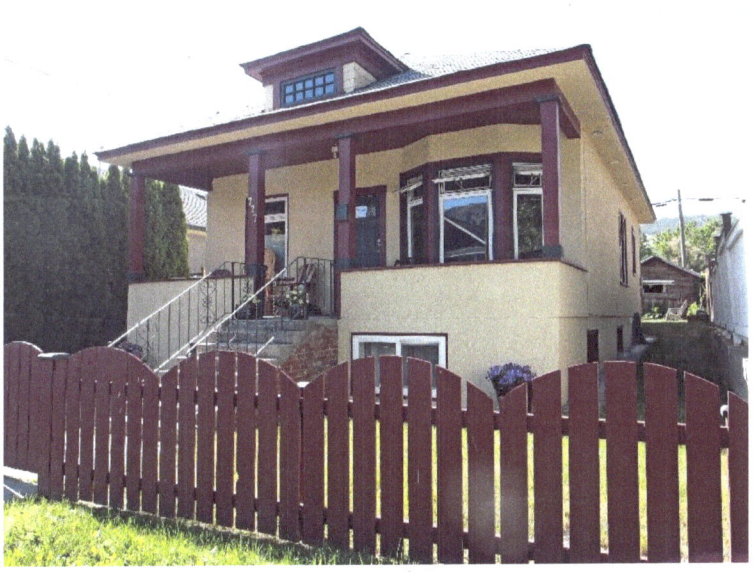

727 St. Paul Street

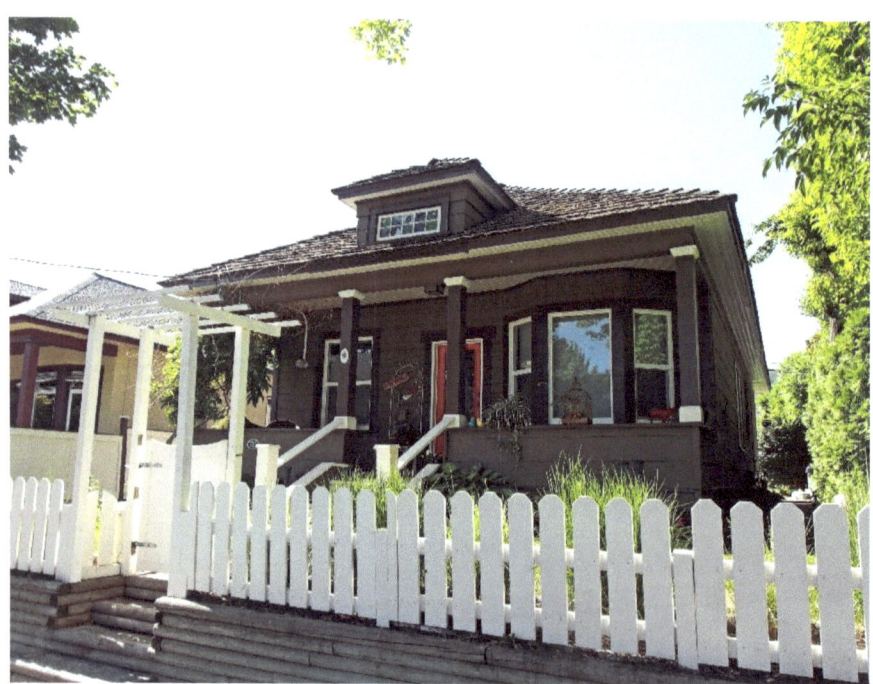

721 St. Paul Street - This is another Craftsman style house and it was built by the same English contractor (as #715) in 1913. Although some of the cedar shingle siding has been covered by asbestos shingle the house has sufficient clapboard siding to retain its heritage character. Typically, it has wood frame windows and a verandah with four square pillars.

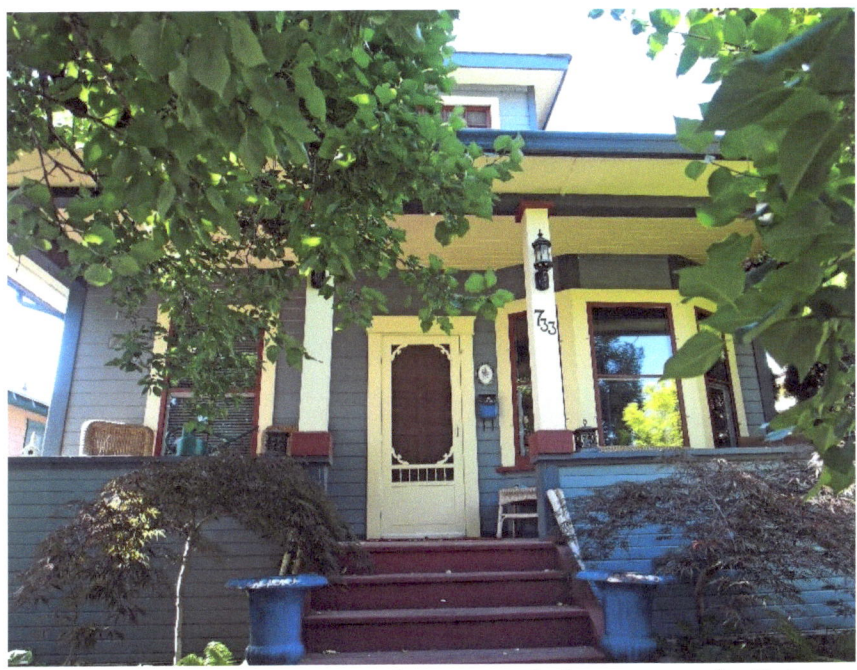

733 St. Paul Street - This Craftsman style house was built in 1915. The exterior features cedar shingles, clapboard siding and original front windows. The verandah has wood plank flooring, clapboard siding and square pillars. The interior has some original doors and fir floors.

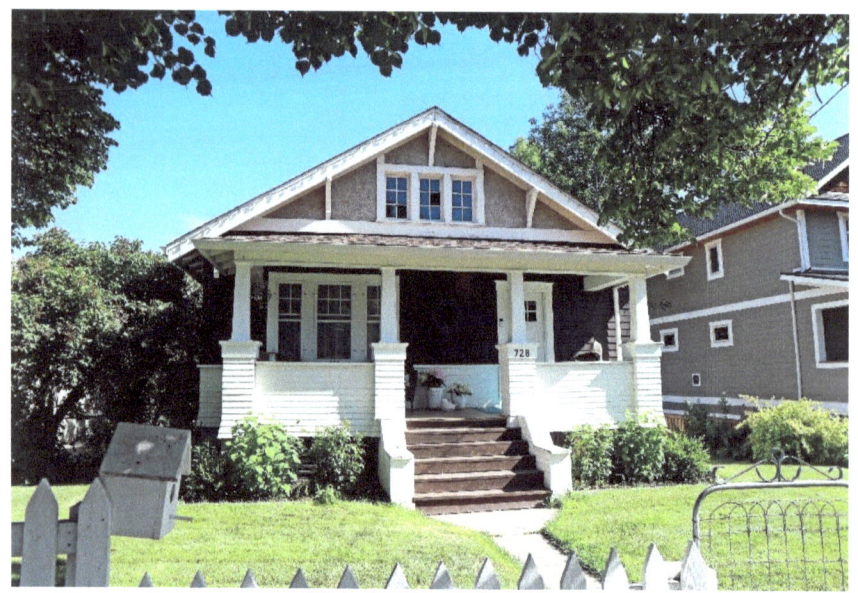

728 St. Paul Street

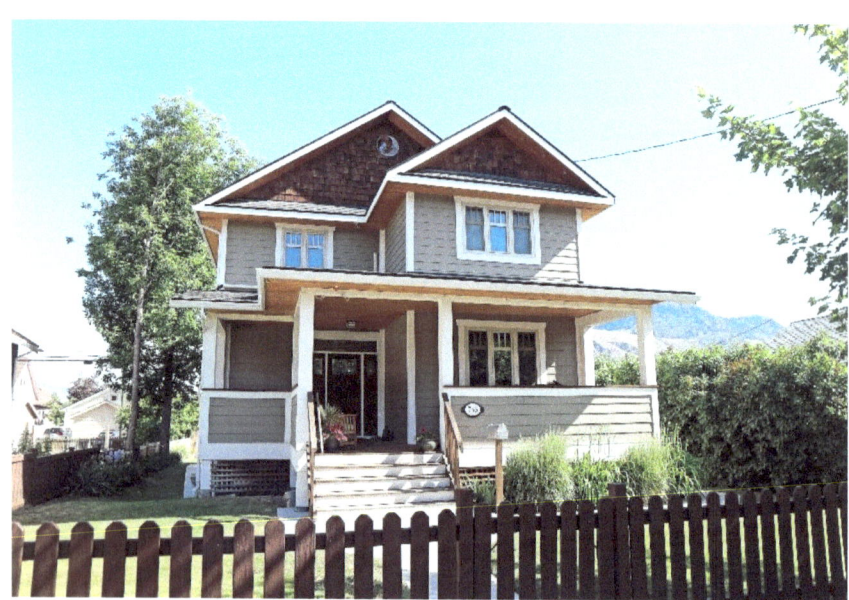

736 St. Paul Street

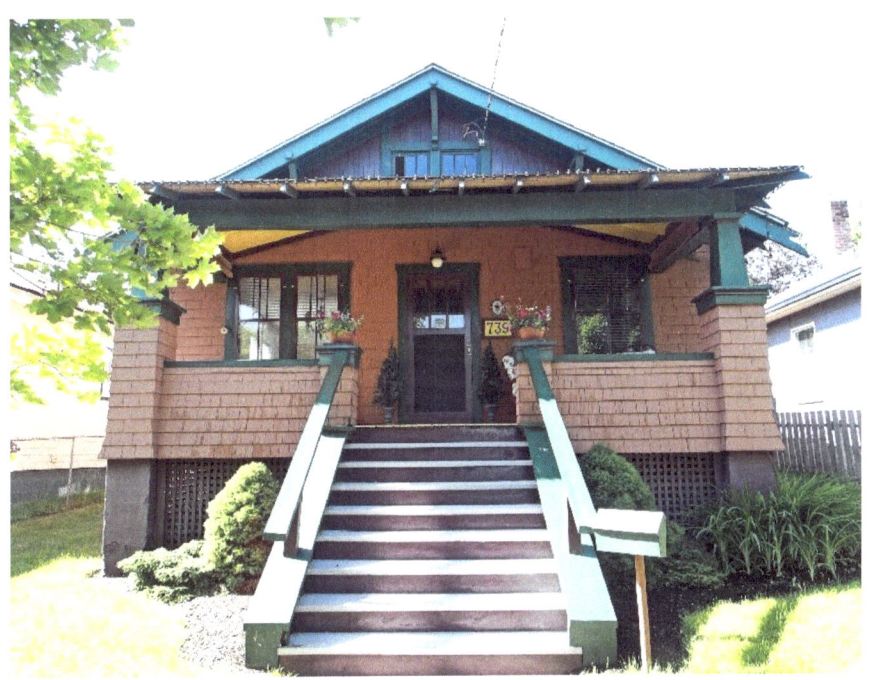

739 St. Paul Street - This Craftsman style house built in 1922 has many original features including v board soffits, wood rafter fascia, cedar shingle siding, multi-pane wood windows and original front door. The verandah also has square pillars and a wood plank floor.

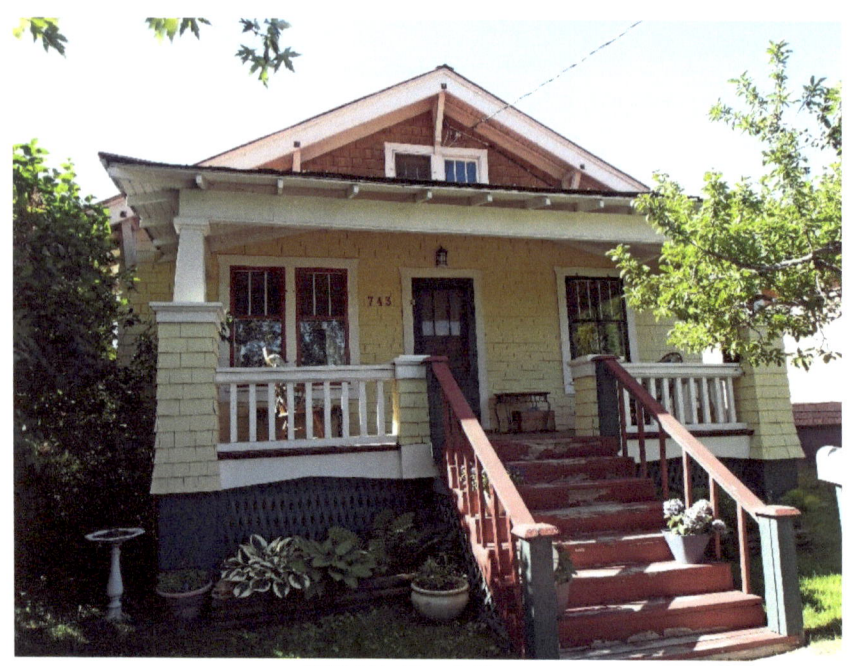
743 St. Paul Street

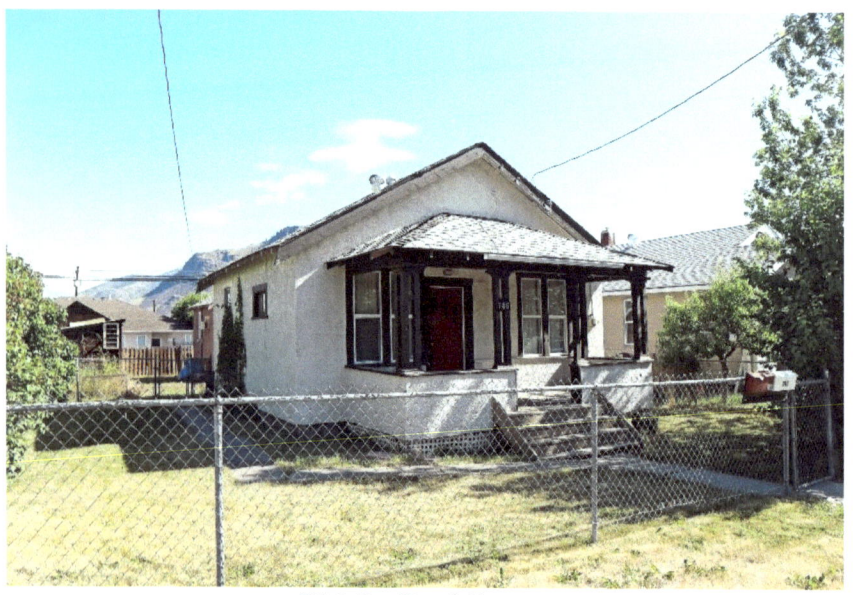
746 St. Paul Street

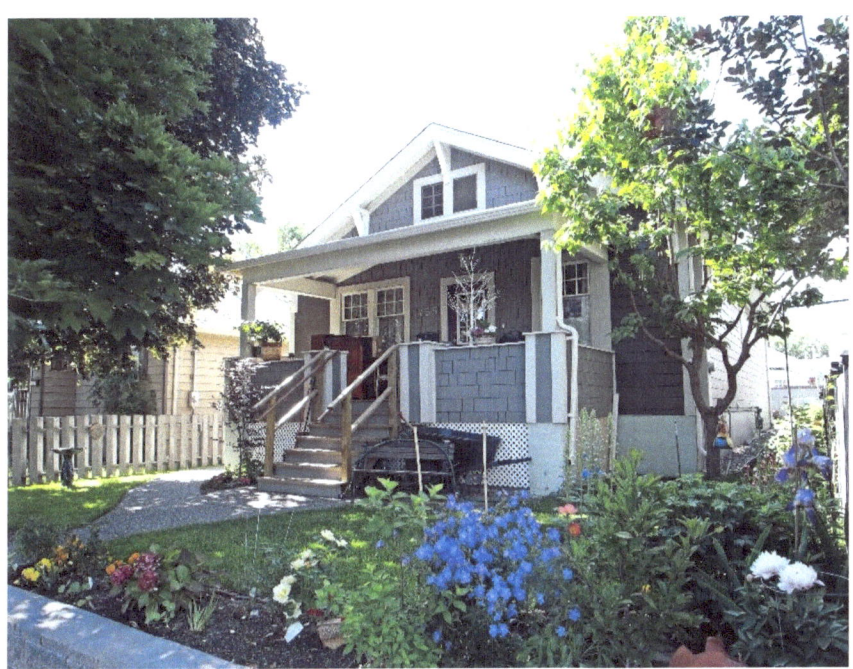

755 St. Paul Street - Another good example of the Craftsman style built in 1923. Original features include v board soffits, wood rafter fascia, cedar shingle siding, multi-pane wood windows and front door. The verandah has square pillars and a wood plank floor.

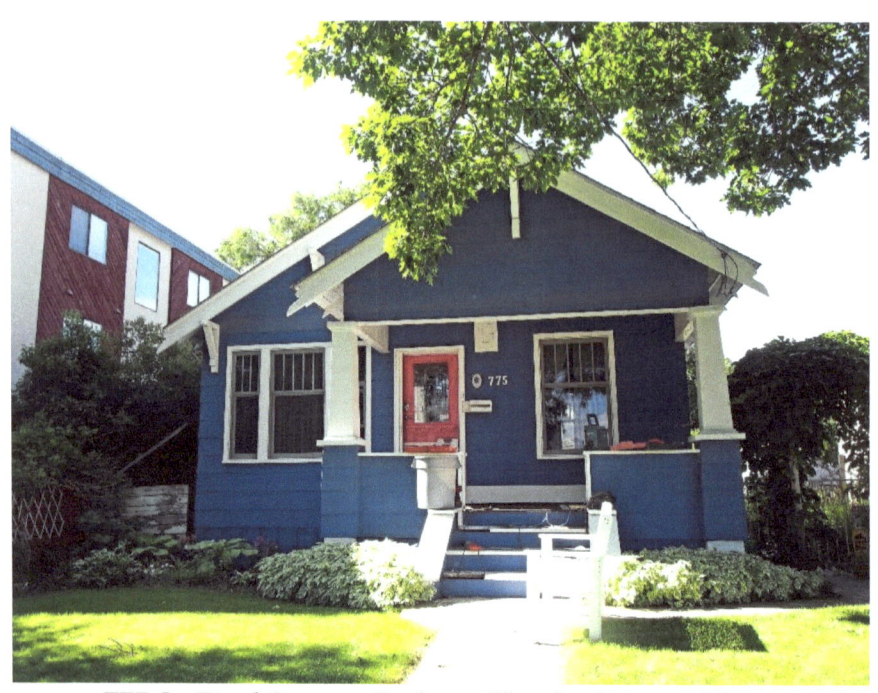

775 St. Paul Street - Sydney Charles Burton House - He was a feisty Kamloops businessman who was also an active member of many public boards as well as a politician. Burton was a real estate agent. In his spare time, he was secretary of the Magic Grater Company. In 1904, Burton was elected alderman by acclamation. Burton was elected as alderman again in 1912 and 1913 and was also elected president of the Conservative Association. Burton was elected president of the Board of Trade (Chamber of Commerce) in 1915 and successfully ran for mayor in 1920 and again in 1921 and 1922.

The house contains many highly typical Craftsman style details. From the pyramid columns on the front verandah, to the front door, multipaned windows, barge boards, and exposed rafters, this house says 1920s. It is late in the decade as is evidenced by the shrinking size of the front verandah.

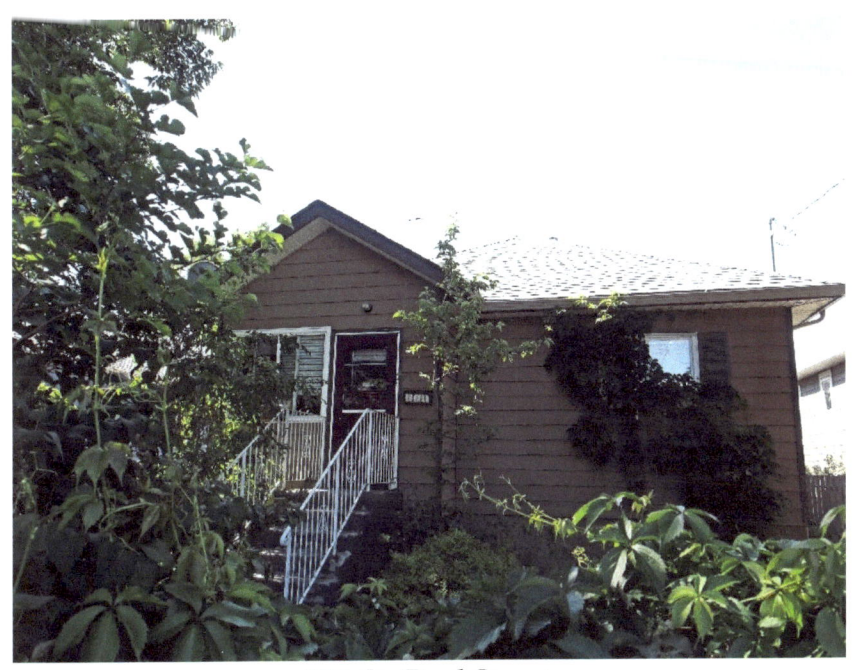

771 St. Paul Street

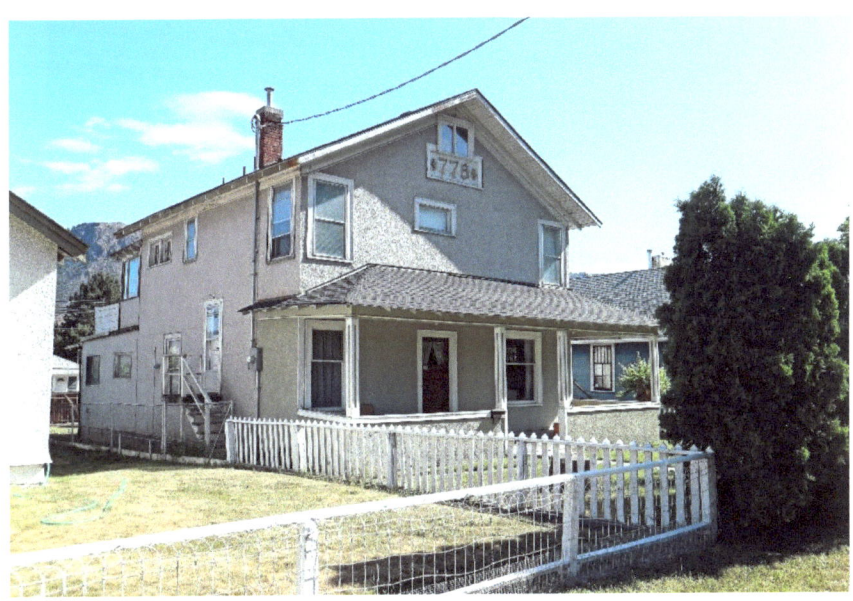

778 St. Paul Street

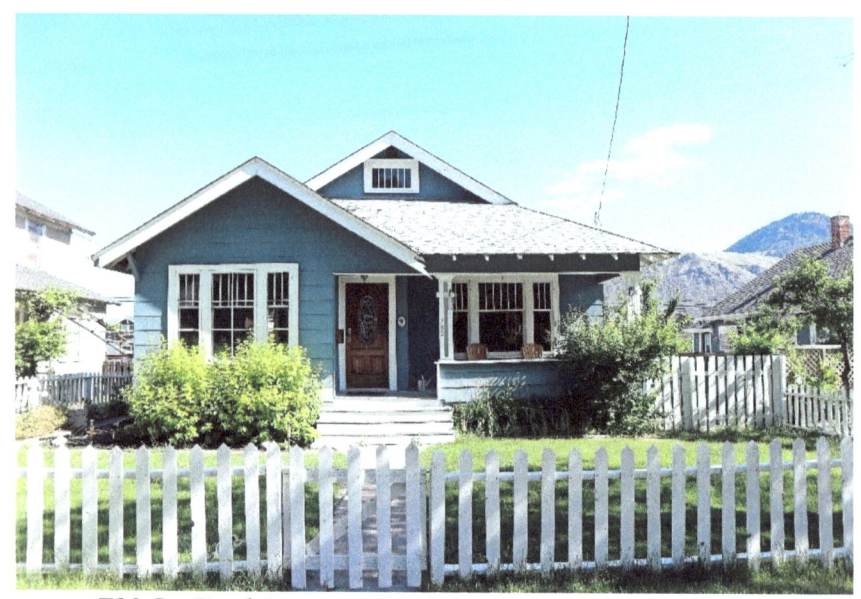

780 St. Paul Street - The Martin Laurence Dohm House - In 1929 C.N.R. Locomotive Engineer, Martin Laurence Dohm, commissioned Kamloops builders, Taylor & Sons, to build this attractive three-bedroom bungalow. No expense was spared in the construction of this home. The floors are honey oak tongue and groove, and the door and window casings and baseboards are crafted from fine wood. The woodwork has never been painted over and remains in its original condition.

One of the highlights of Mr. Dohm's 44-year career with the C.N.R. was serving as Engineer on the Royal train when Queen Mother Elizabeth and King George VI visited Kamloops in 1939.

One year after moving into their new home, the Dohms built a larger home on the vacant lot right next door at 786 St. Paul Street. Although the living and dining rooms were a respectable size, Mrs. Elizabeth Dohm found the kitchen to be unsuitable for her growing family.

The 'elephantine' porch pillars are unusual and there are multi-pane windows.

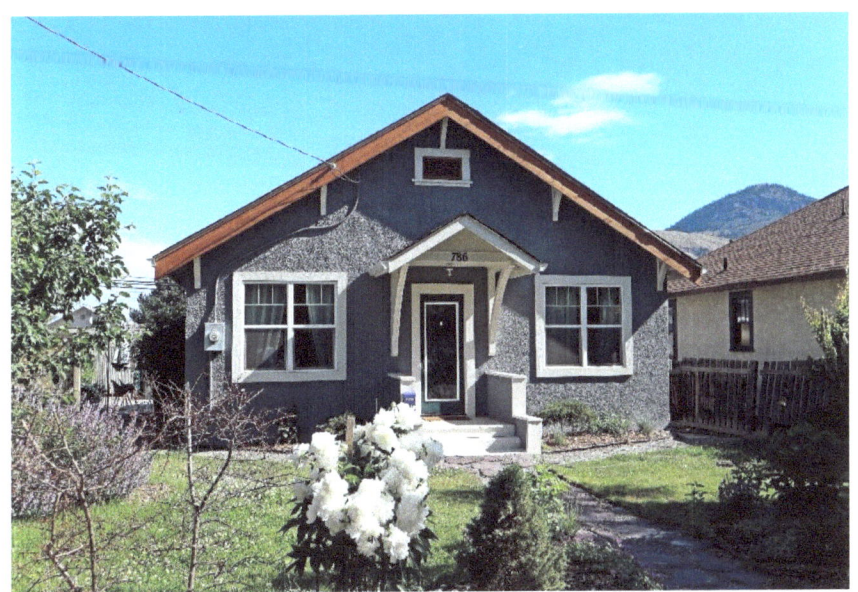

786 St. Paul Street – larger home for the Dohm family than #780

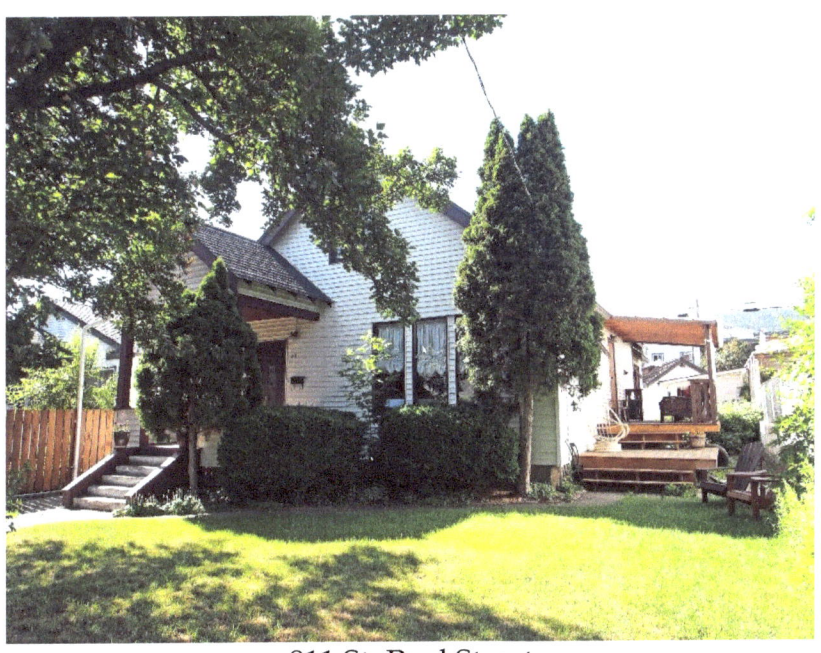

811 St. Paul Street

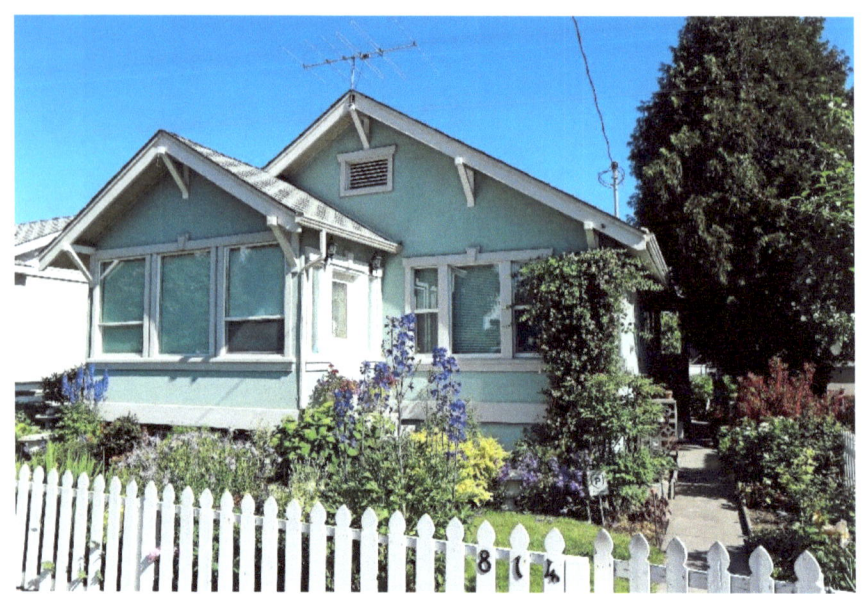
814 St. Paul Street

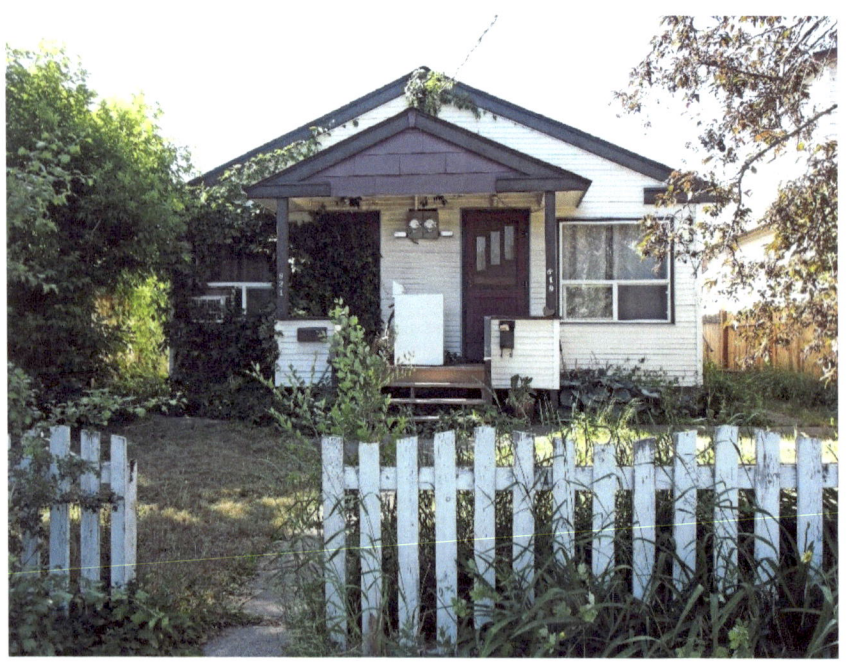
819 St. Paul Street

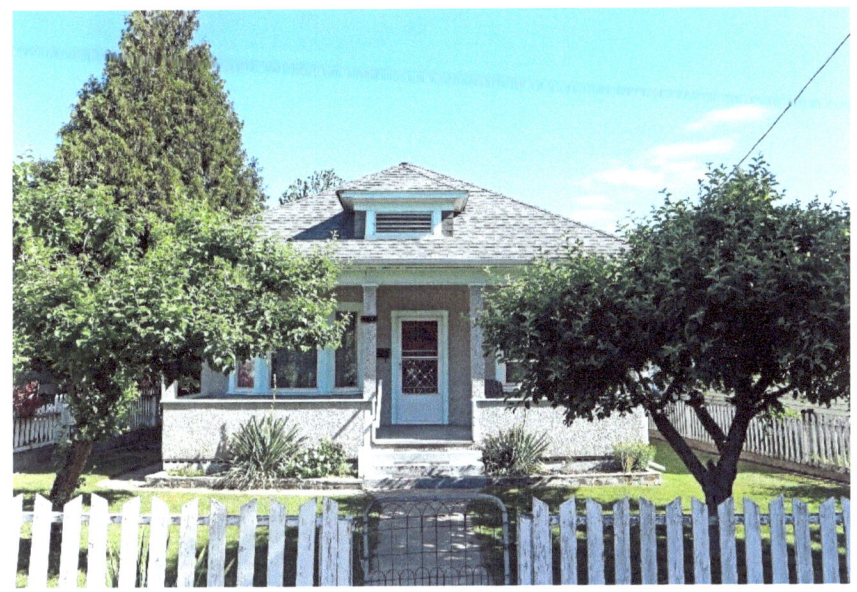

822 St. Paul Street

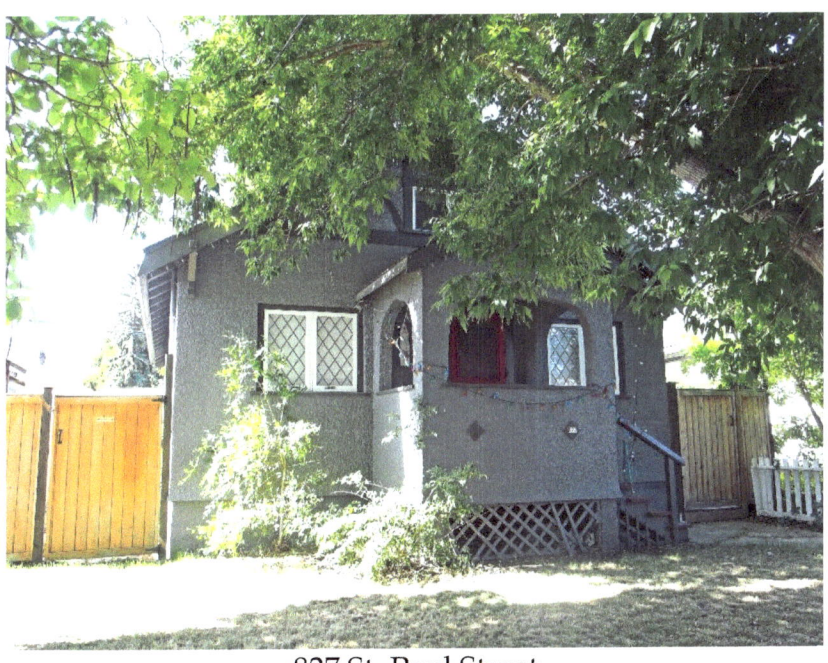

827 St. Paul Street

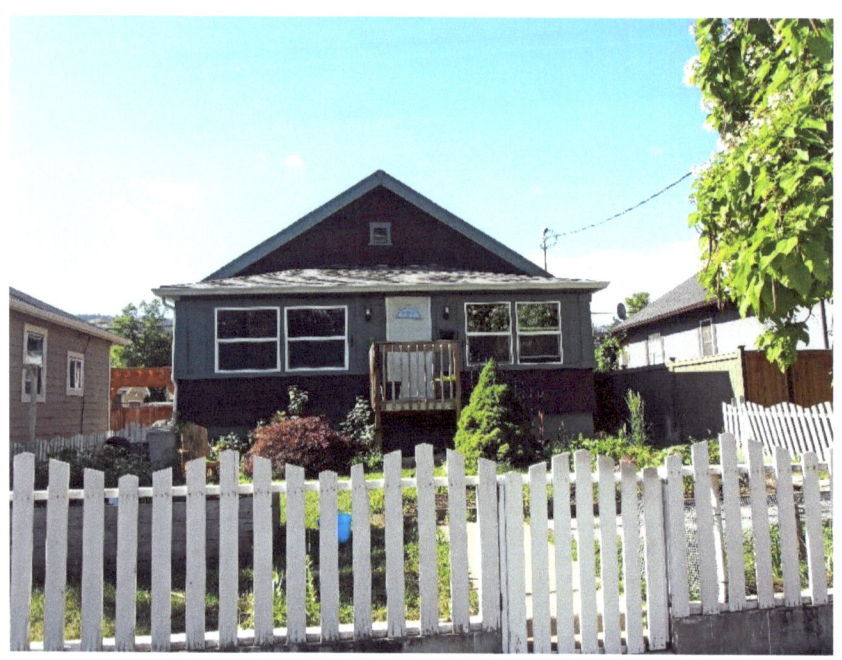

833 St. Paul Street

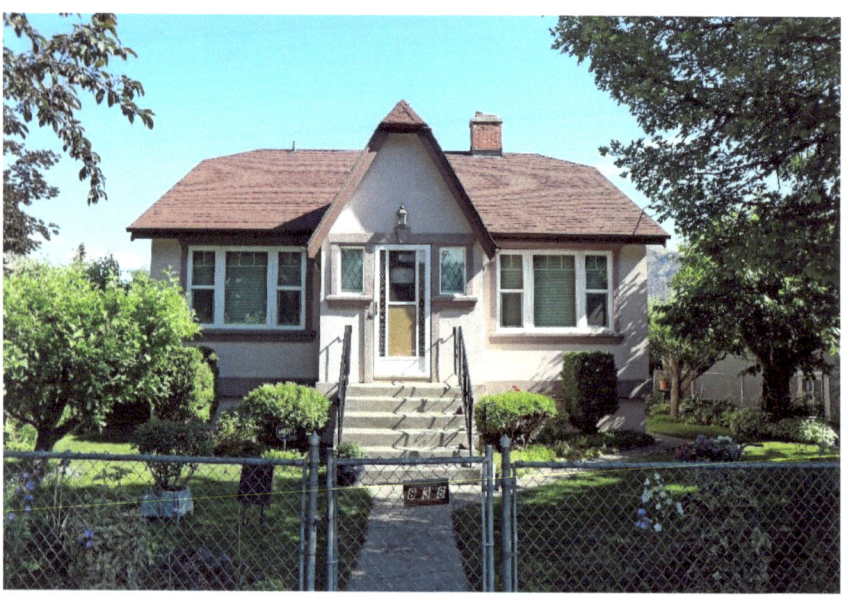

836 St. Paul Street

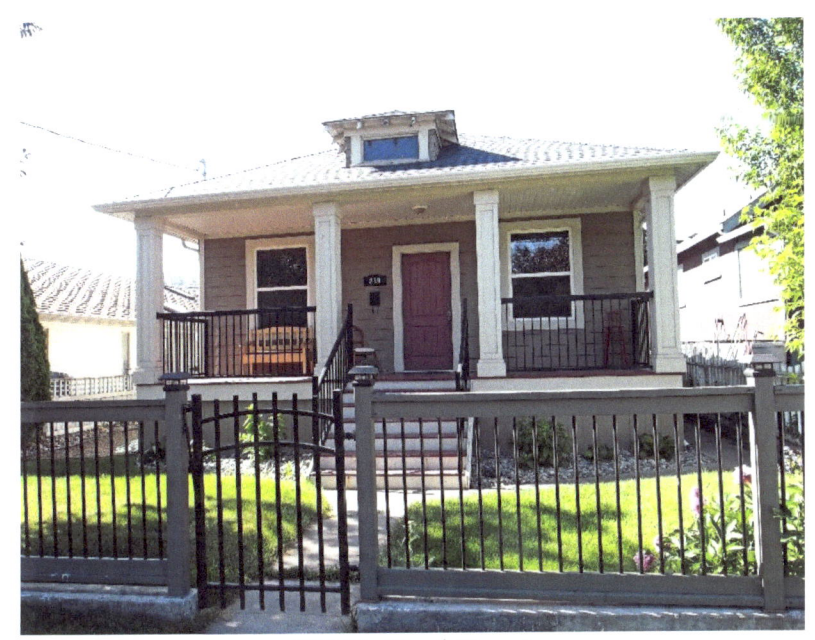
839 St. Paul Street

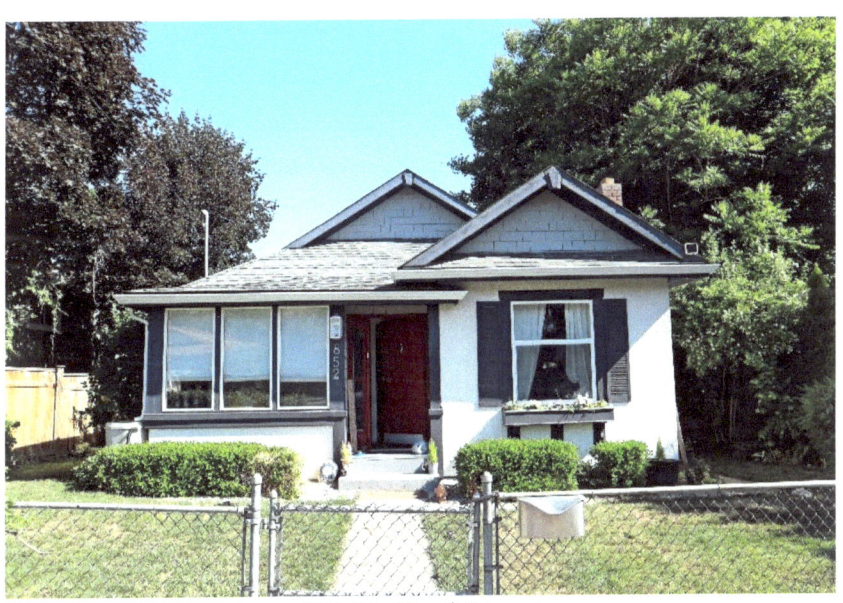
852 St. Paul Street

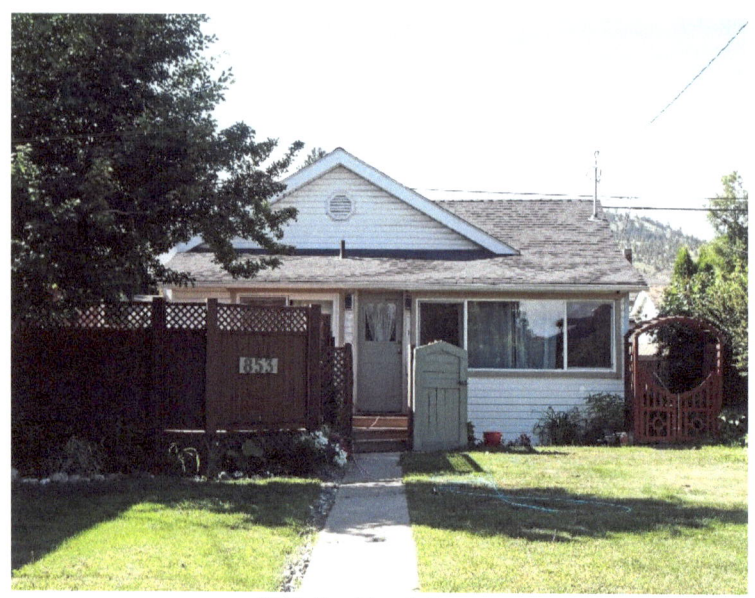

853 St. Paul Street

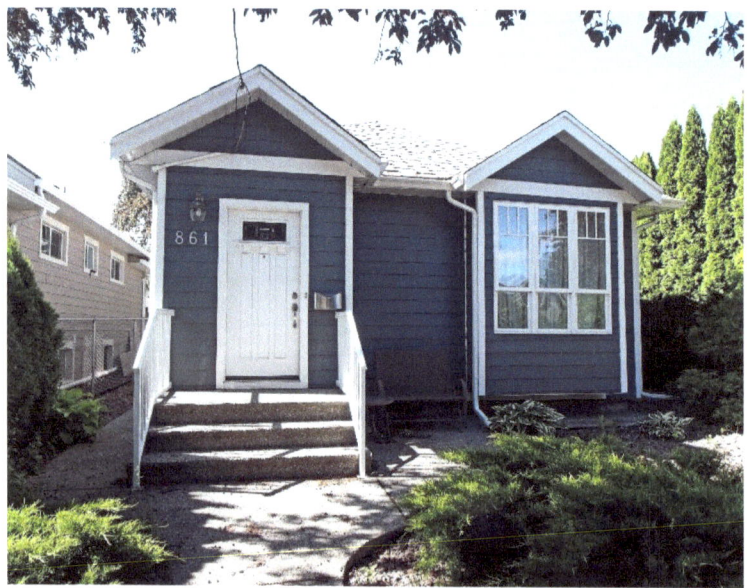

861 St. Paul Street

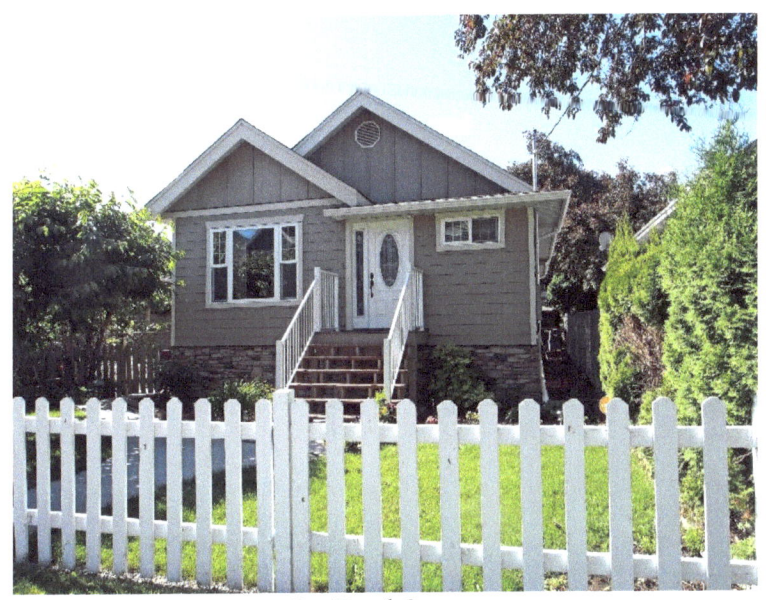

St. Paul Street

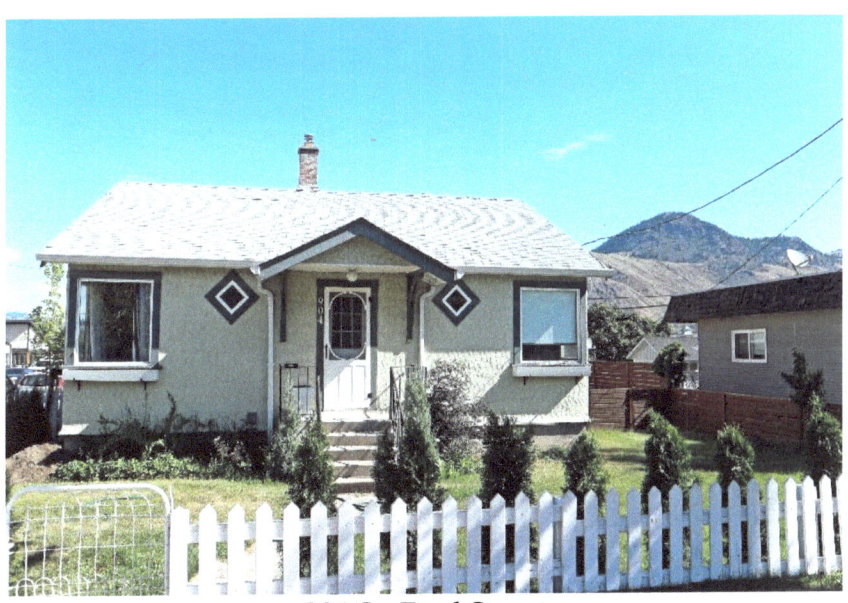

904 St. Paul Street

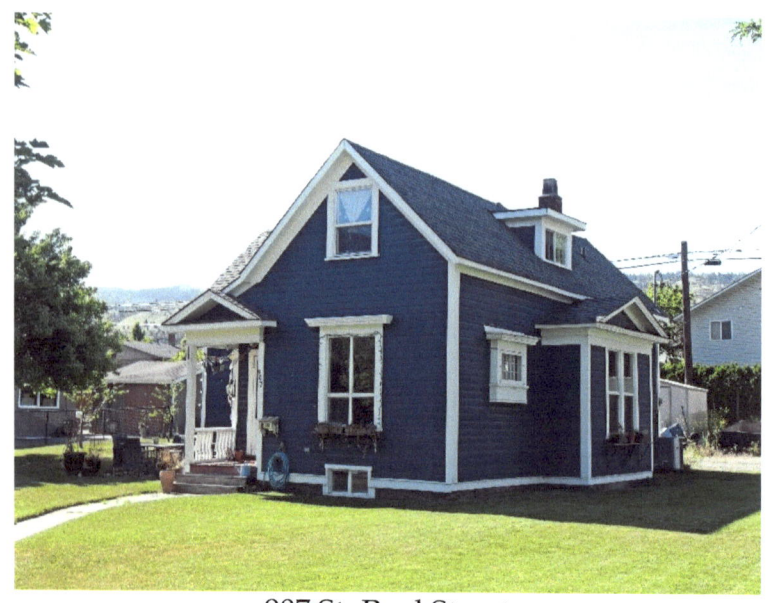

907 St. Paul Street

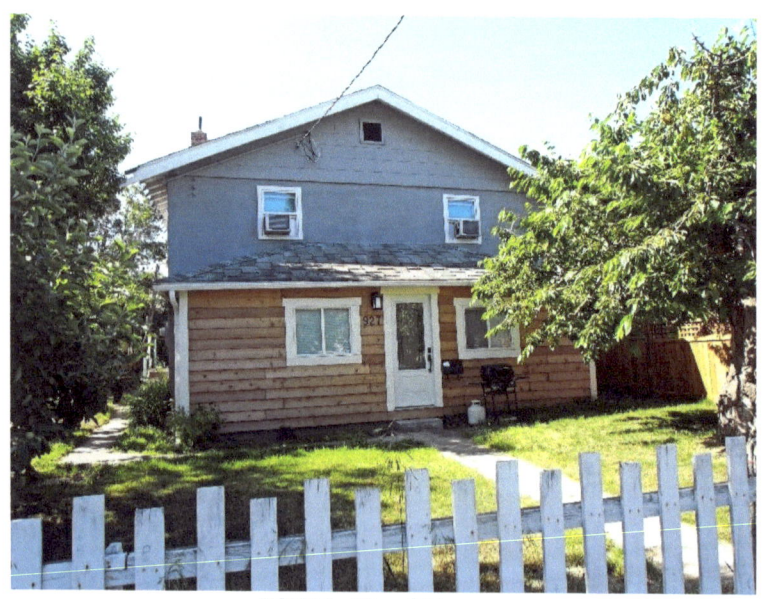

927 St. Paul Street

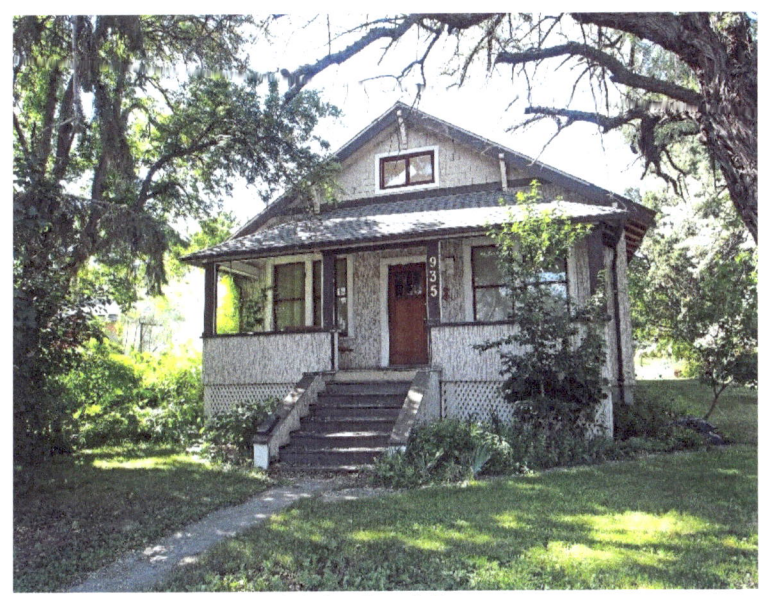

935 St. Paul Street

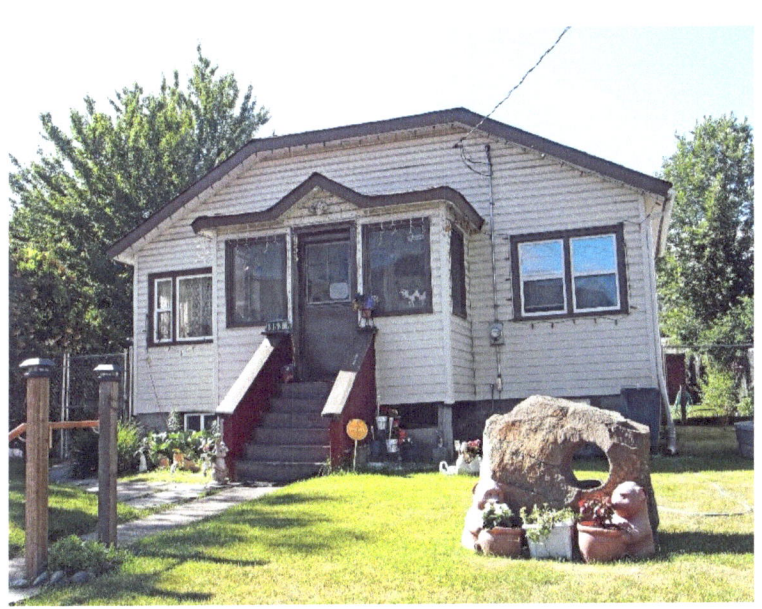

953 St. Paul Street

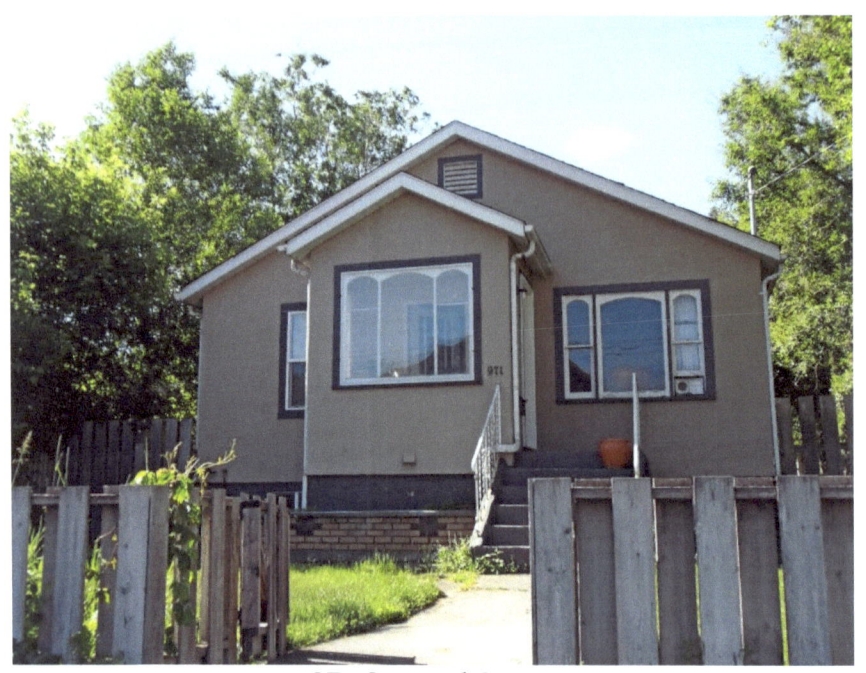

971 St. Paul Street

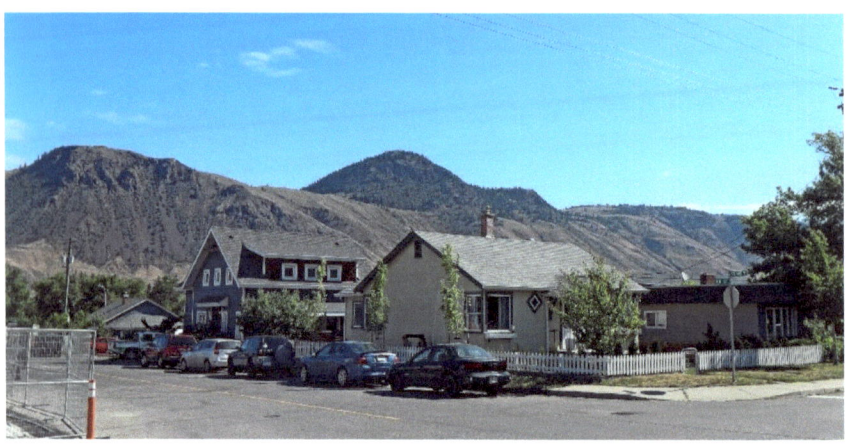

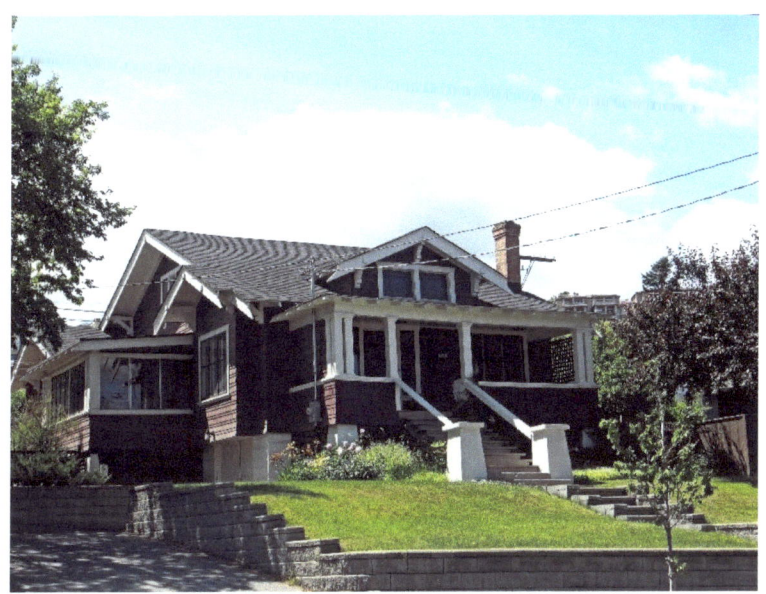

119 Battle Street

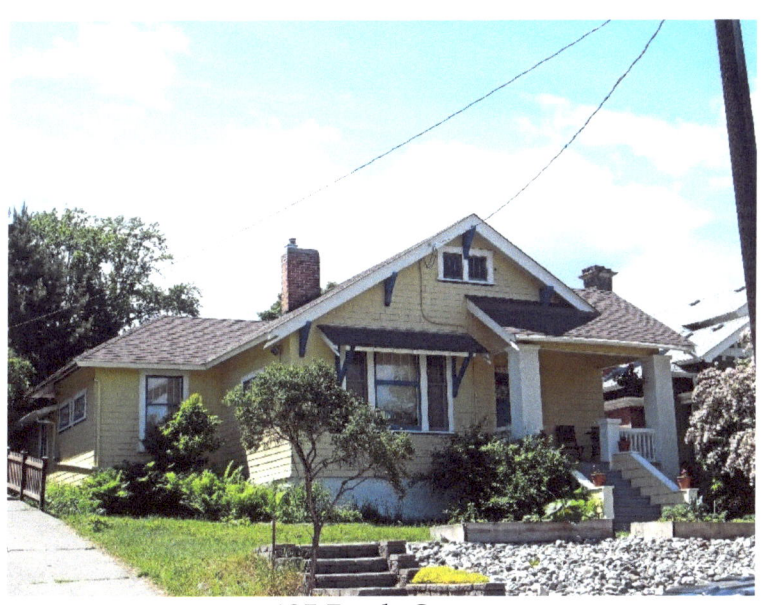

135 Battle Street

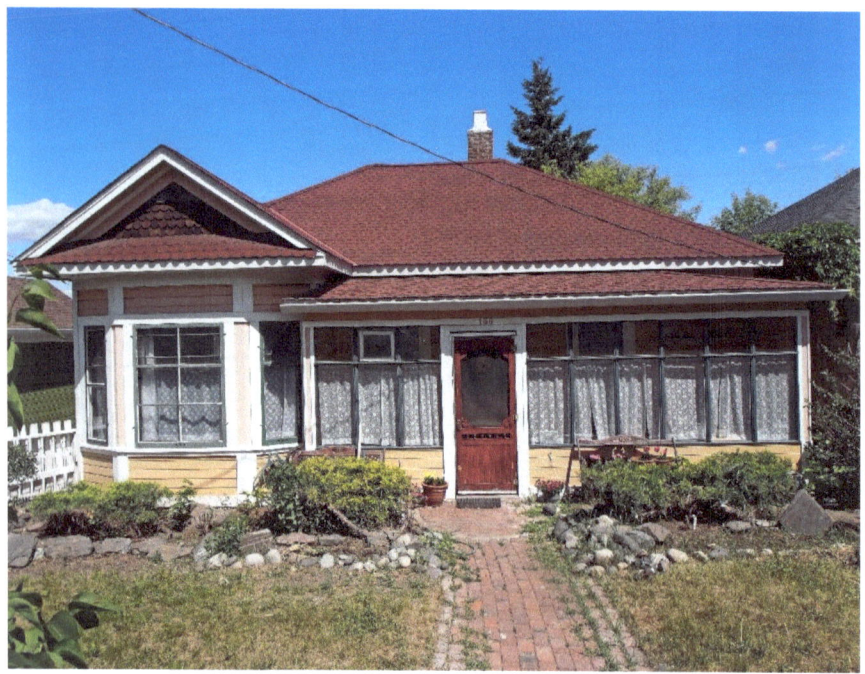

136 Battle Street - The style of this house is described as a Bungalow and built in 1906. It has original clapboard siding, soffits, fascia, multi-pane windows, some with frosted glass, and an enclosed veranda.

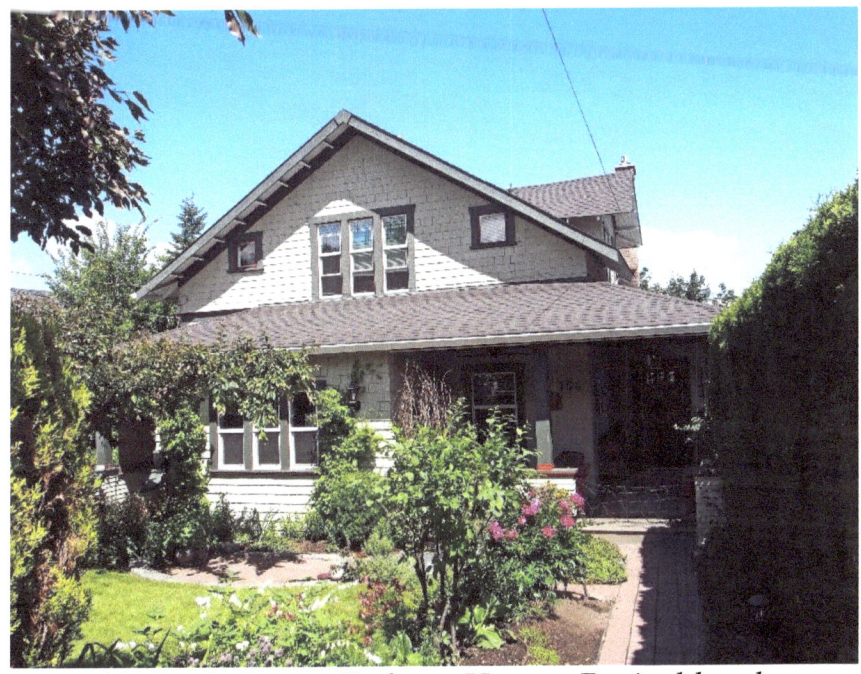

154 Battle Street - Bethune House - Reginald and Marion Bethune built this house in 1913 and occupied it for thirty-two years. Reginald was an Imperial Bank manager, the Provincial Tax Collector, President of the Native Sons of Canada, served as Board Chairman of the Royal Inland Hospital, and greeted the Duke and Duchess of Connaught at the hospital's opening in 1912. Marion was an active member of the Ladies' Auxiliary to the Royal Inland Hospital in 1916 and its vice-president in 1918.

Original exterior features of this Craftsman style house include cedar shingle and wood siding, brick foundation, leaded glass windows, and full verandah wrapping the back and side of the house.

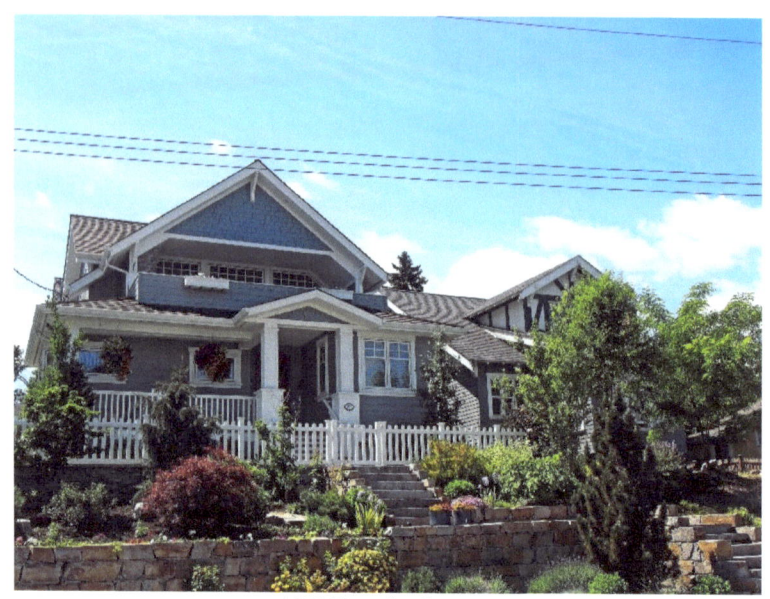
155 Battle Street

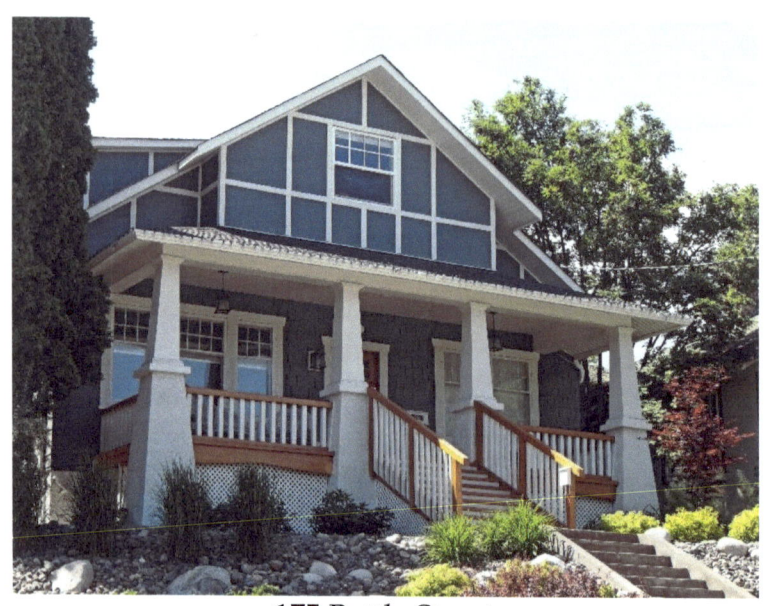
175 Battle Street

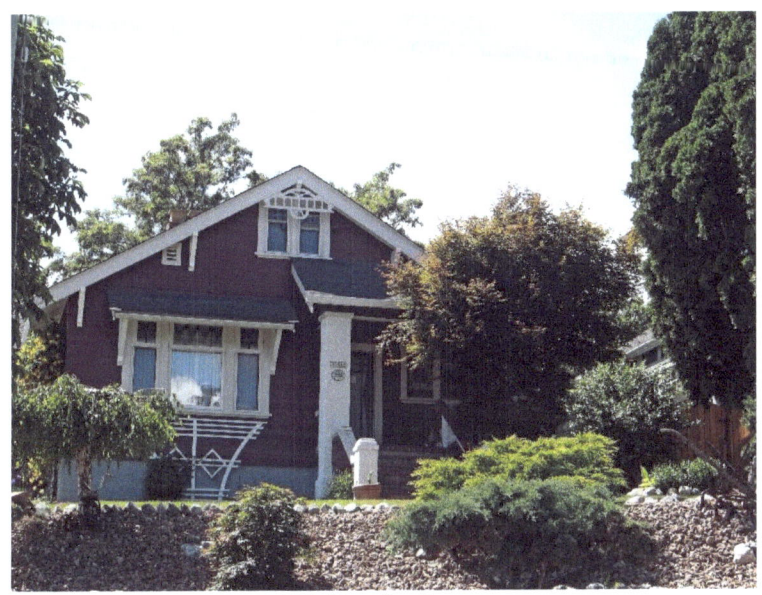

183 Battle Street

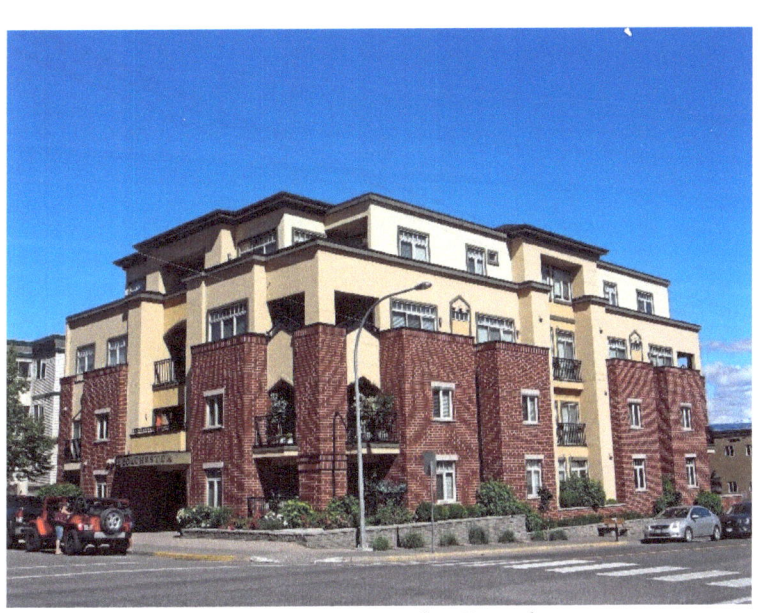

370 Battle Street – The Dorchester

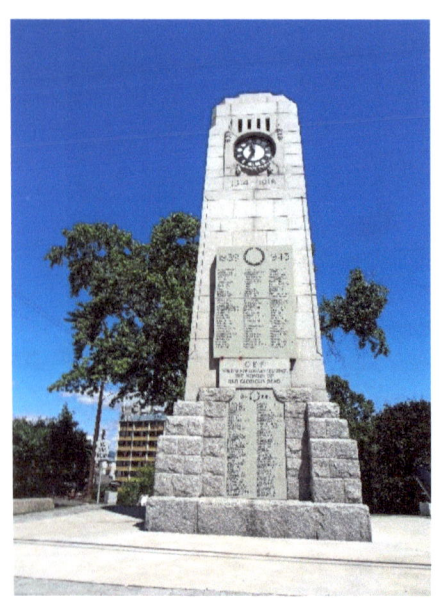 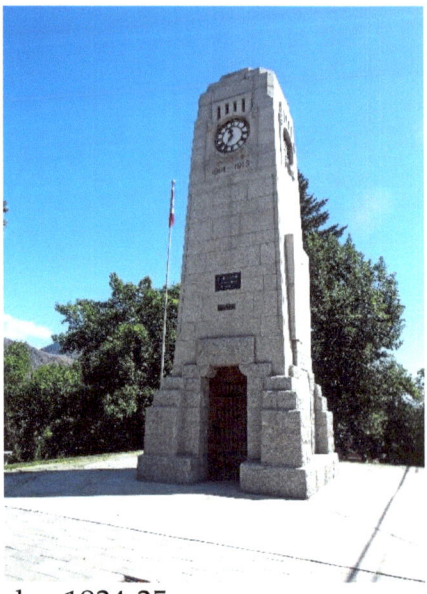

Memorial Park – 1924-25

Shortly after World War I ended, the Women's Auxiliary of the Canadian Legion began raising funds for a war memorial. The cenotaph was built, the gardens were developed and the trees were planted as living memorials to the soldiers who died. The cairn was dedicated to the students of Stuart Wood School who died in war.

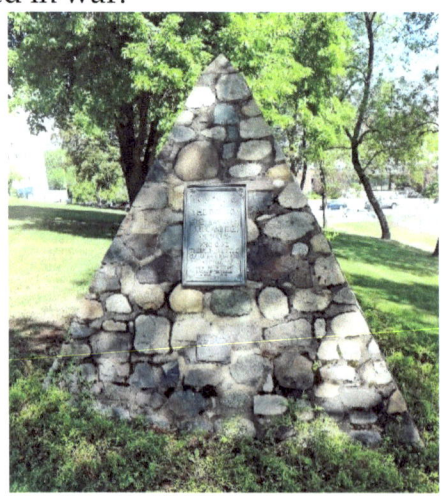

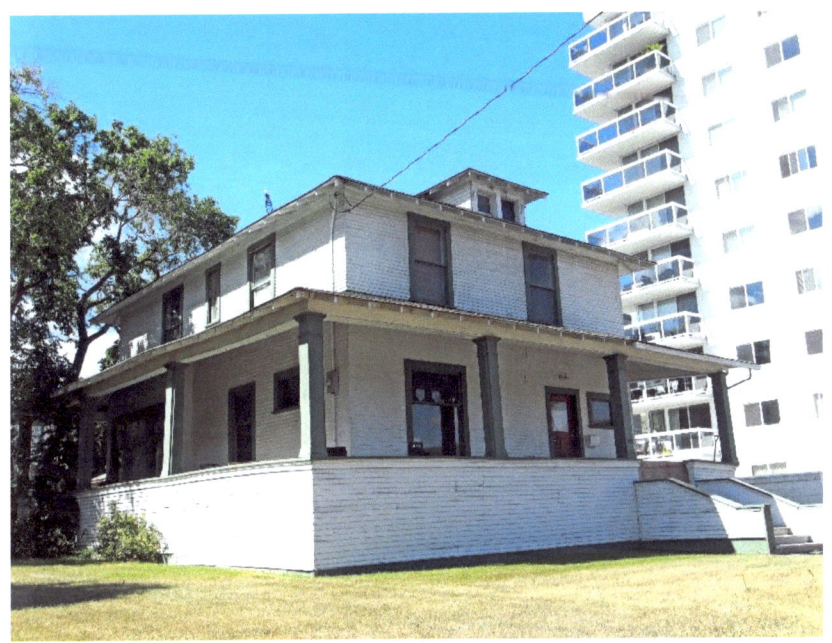

435 Battle Street

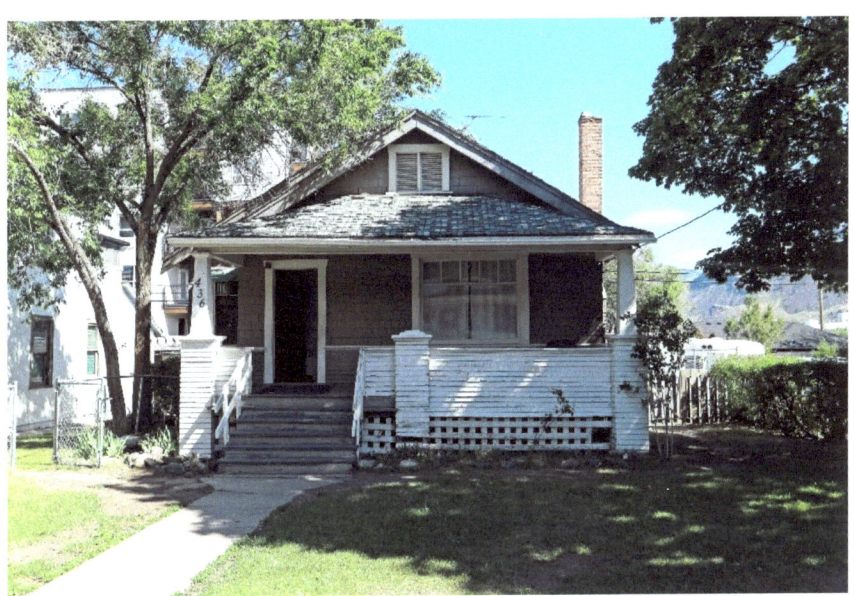

436 Battle Street

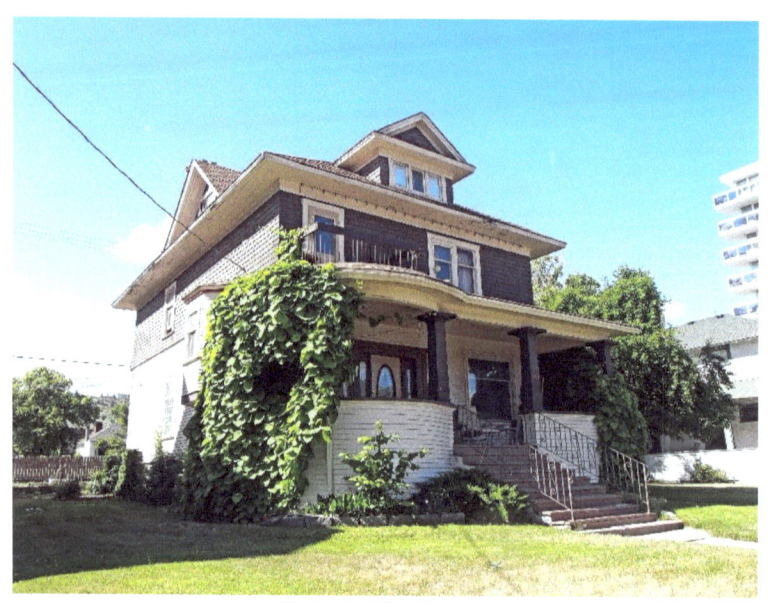

451 Battle Street

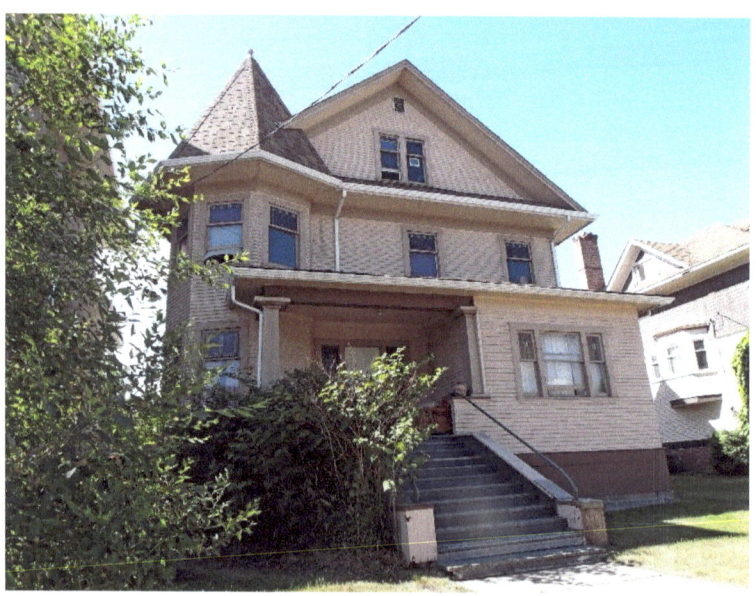

Battle Street

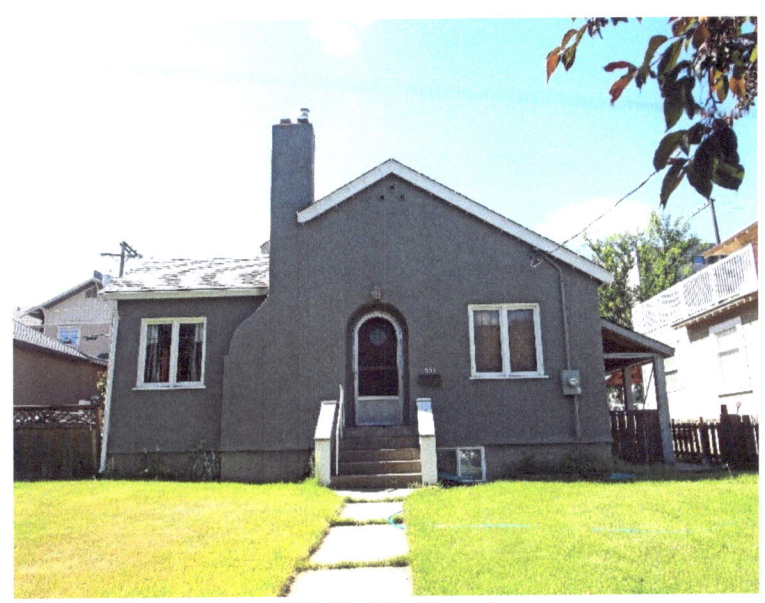

551 Battle Street

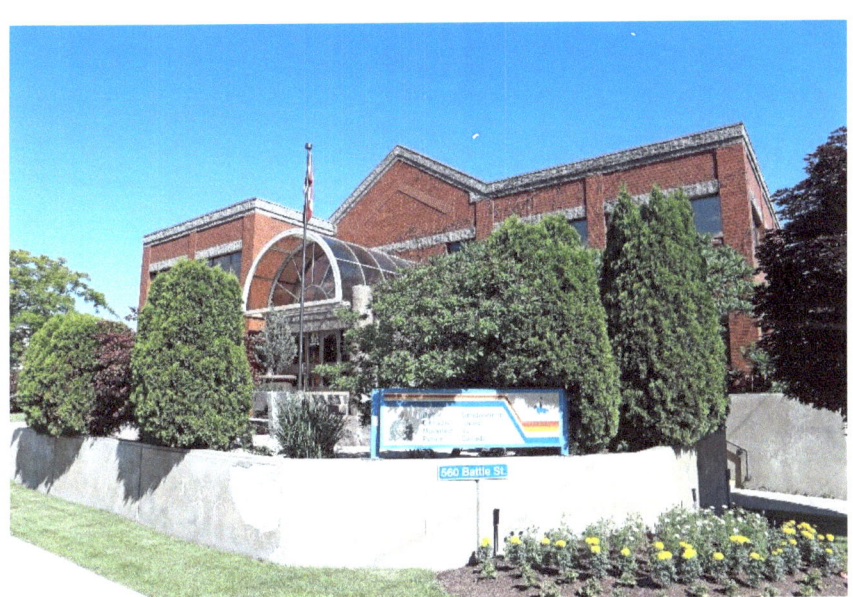

560 Battle Street – Royal Canadian Mounted Police

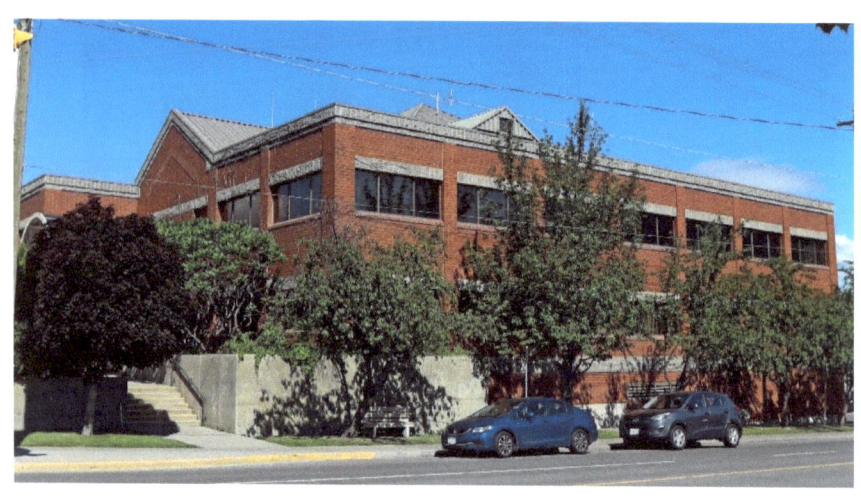

560 Battle Street

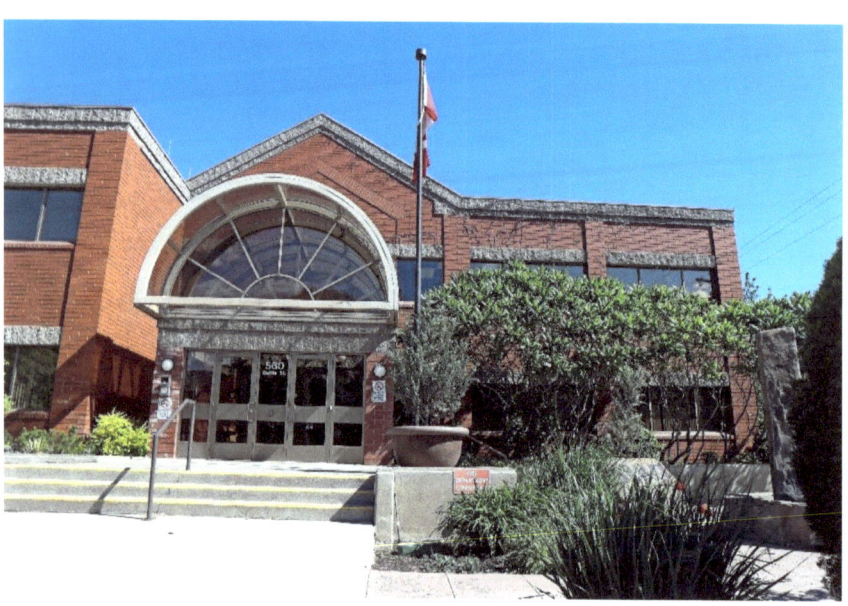

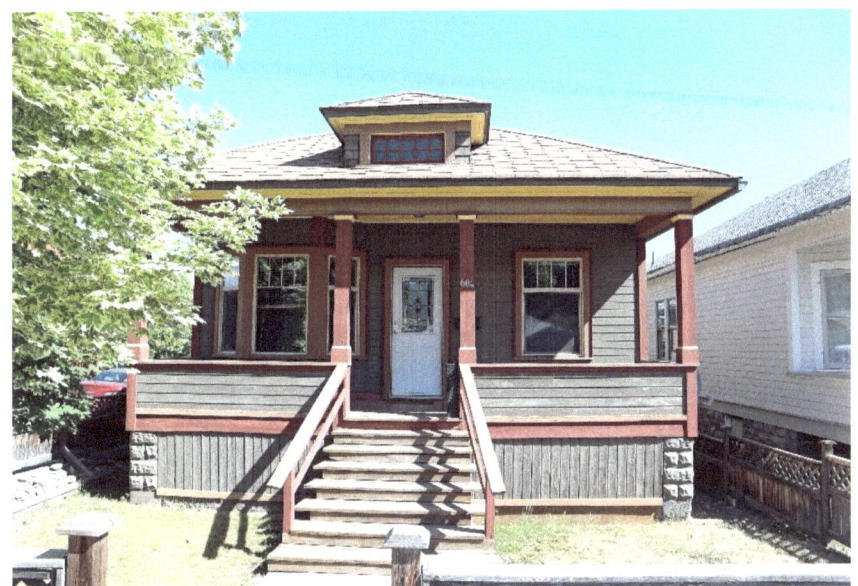

604 Battle Street

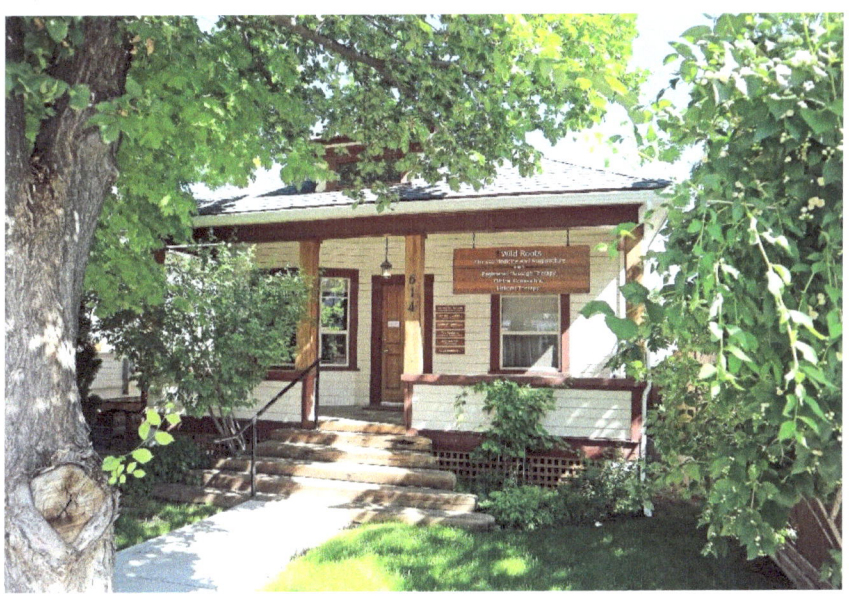

614 Battle Street

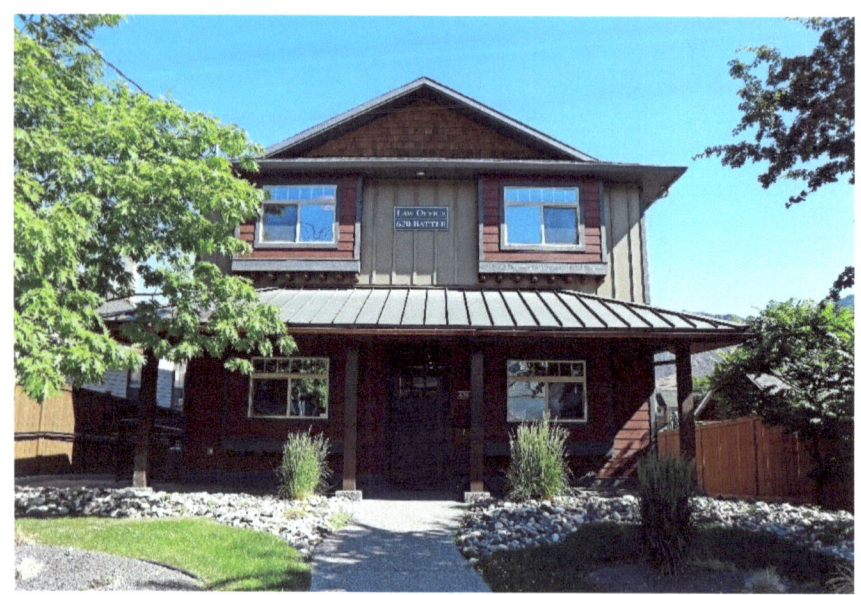

620 Battle Street

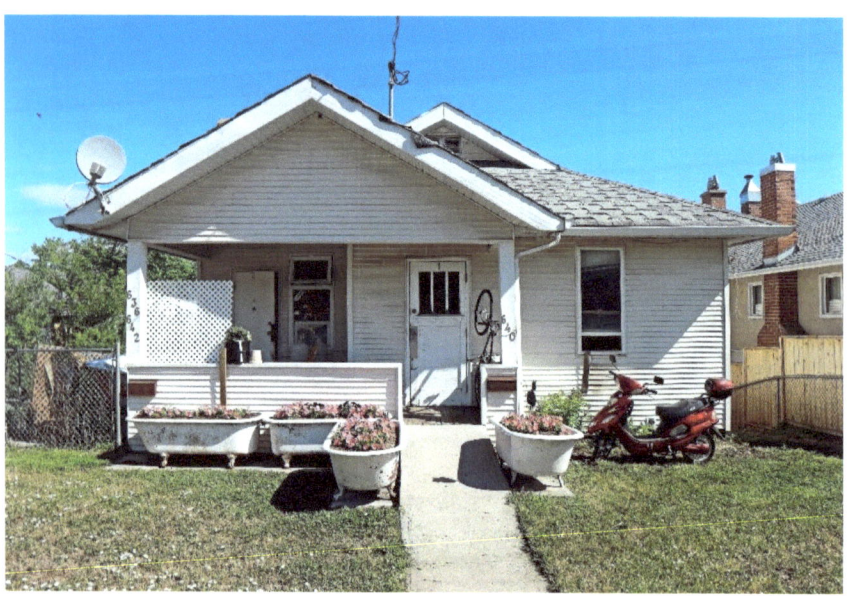

640 Battle Street

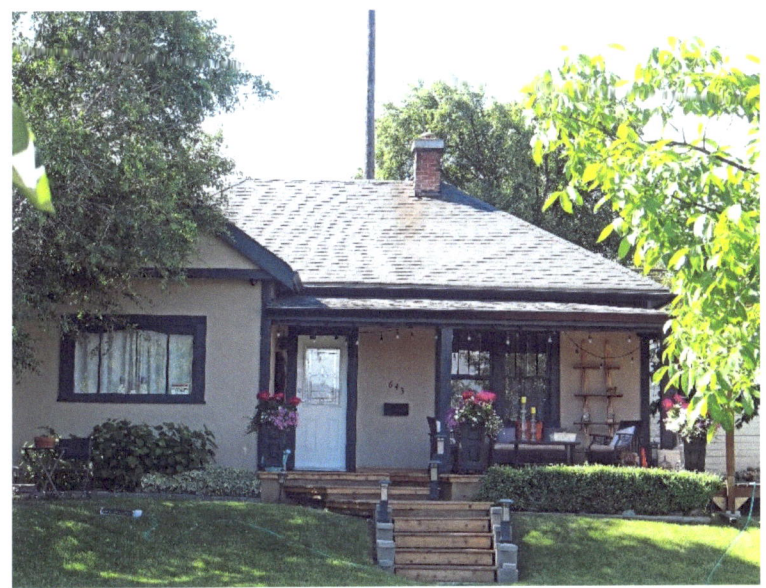

643 Battle Street

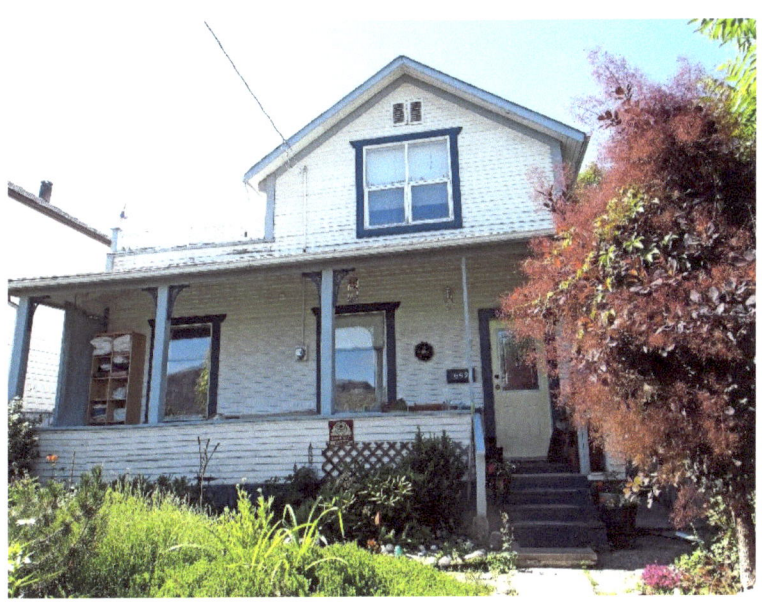

649 Battle Street

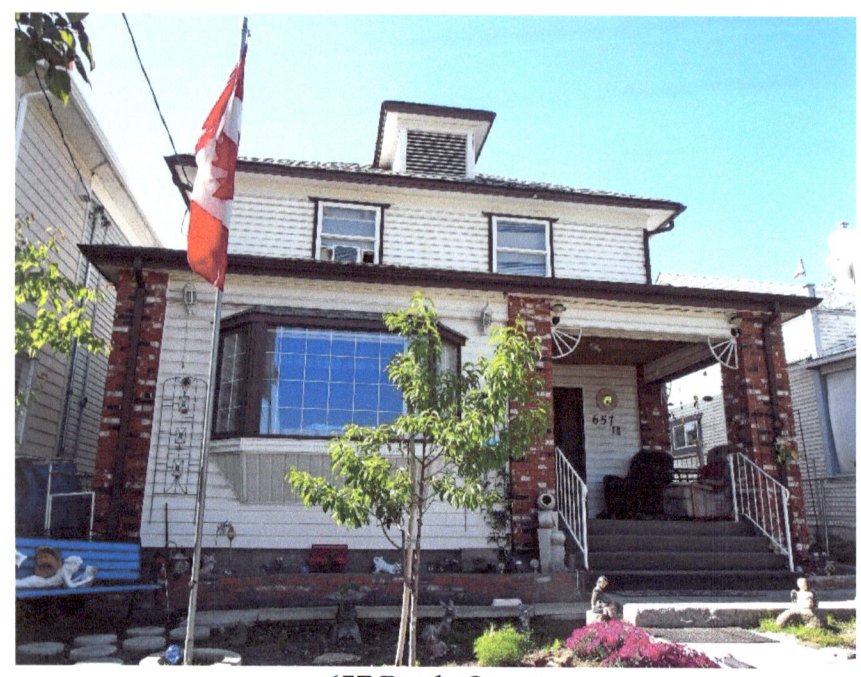
657 Battle Street

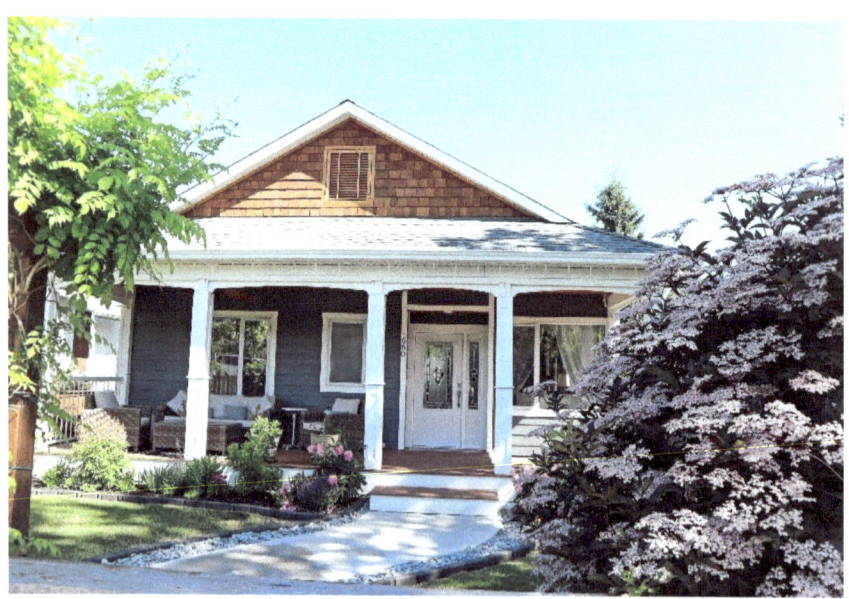
660 Battle Street

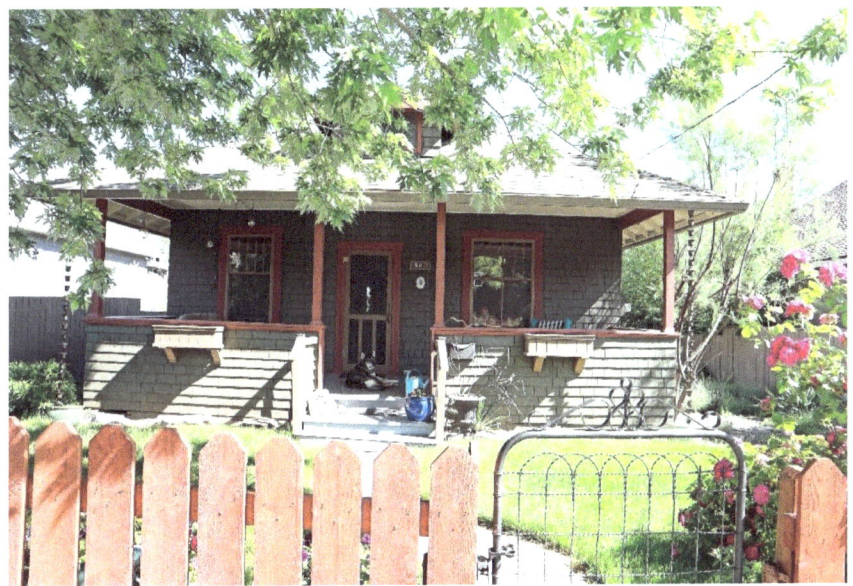

668 Battle Street - This house was built in 1926 in a bungalow style. It features original cedar shingle siding, wood frame multi-pane windows and original front door. The verandah has square pillars and tongue and groove flooring.

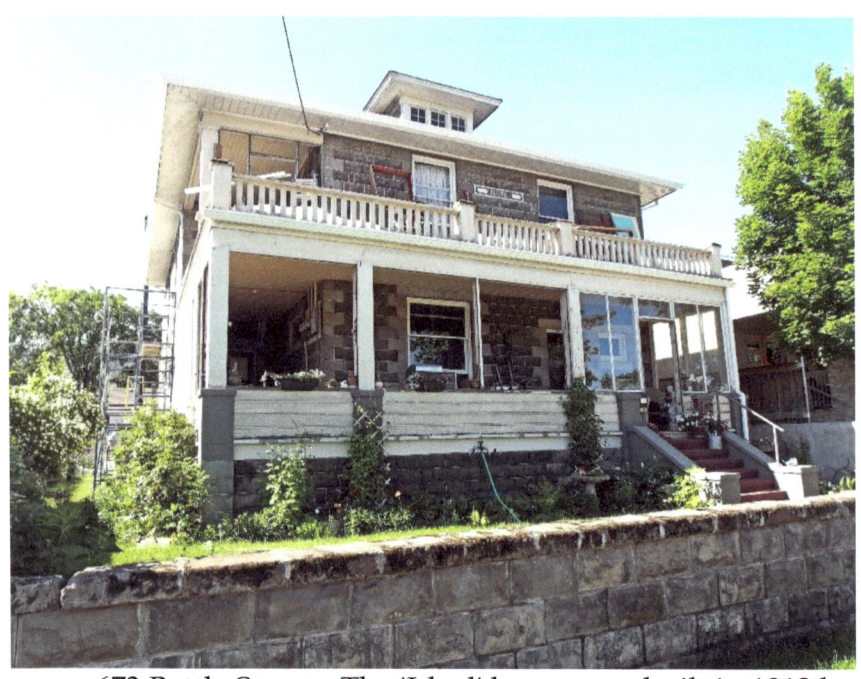

673 Battle Street - The 'Ideal' house was built in 1912 by Edwin and Alice Walkley. Mr. Walkley was the owner of the Small and Dobson Cement Plant in BC Fruitlands on the North Shore. The plant manufactured concrete building blocks which were used to build many basements in Kamloops.

Walkley introduced a molded hollow block to Kamloops called 'ideal' blocks which he used to build this house and one at 467 St. Paul Street. The hollow shape was meant to replace the need for insulation. In fact, the house was cool in the summer, but too cold in the winter. Each block was hand-made by Walkley in the backyard using several molds with different patterns on the facing. The blocks were sundried before being set into place. The overall style of the house is very similar to the wood frame, two storey four-square houses of the same era with attic dormer windows found throughout Kamloops.

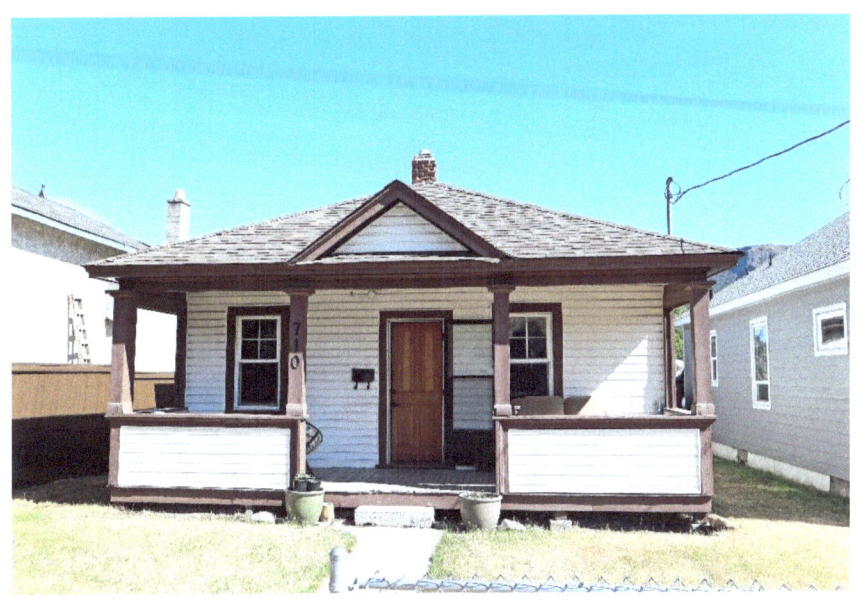

710 Battle Street

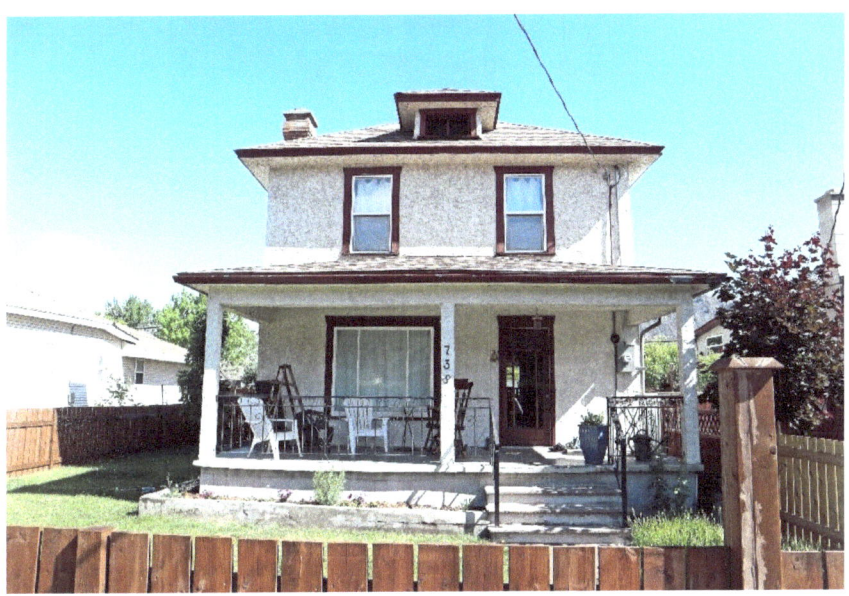

738 Battle Street

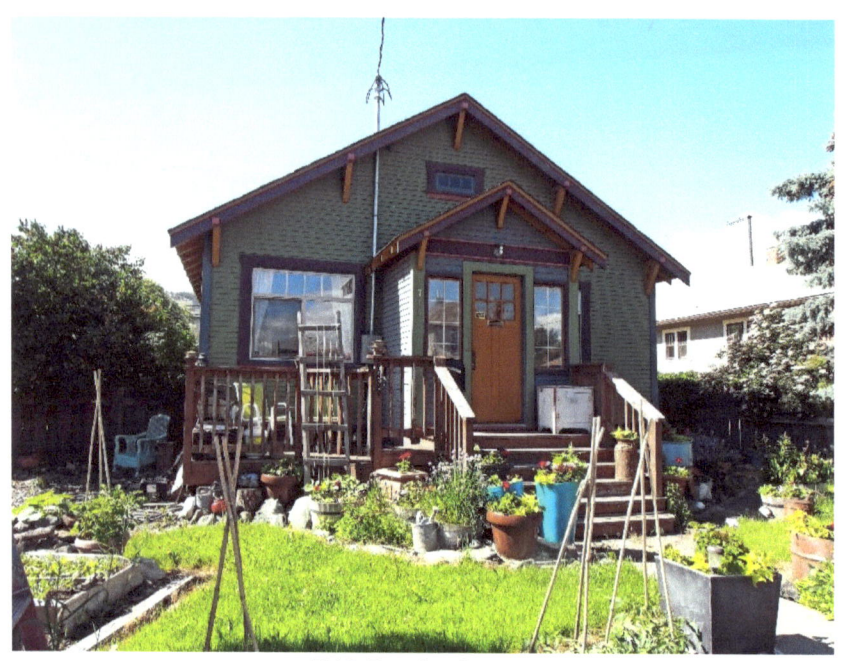

743 Battle Street

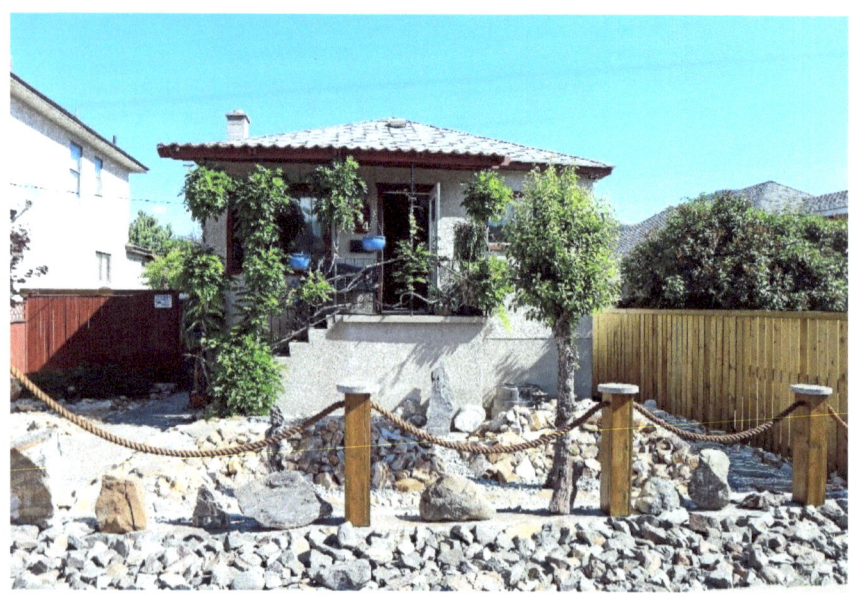

744 Battle Street

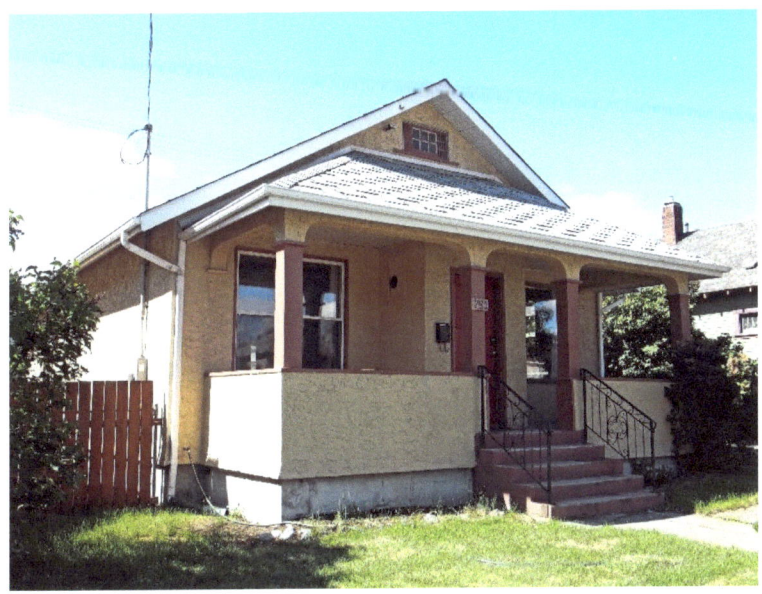

751 Battle Street

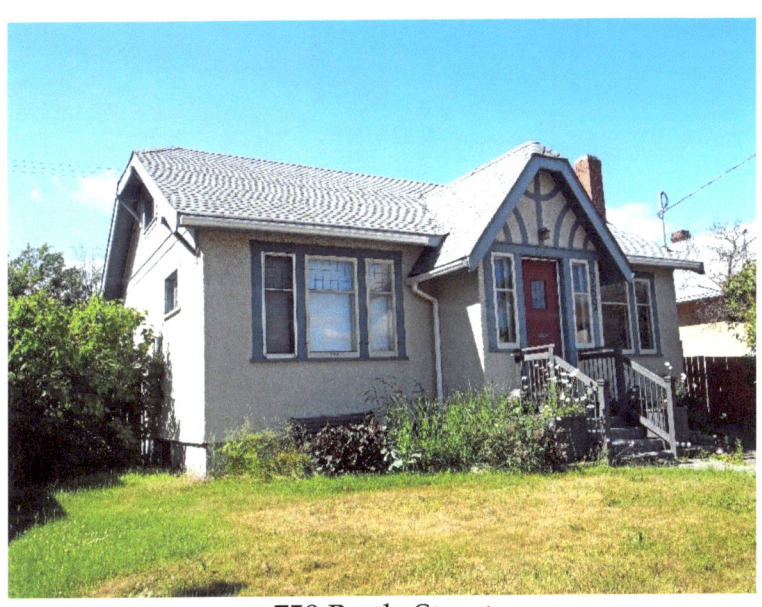

759 Battle Street

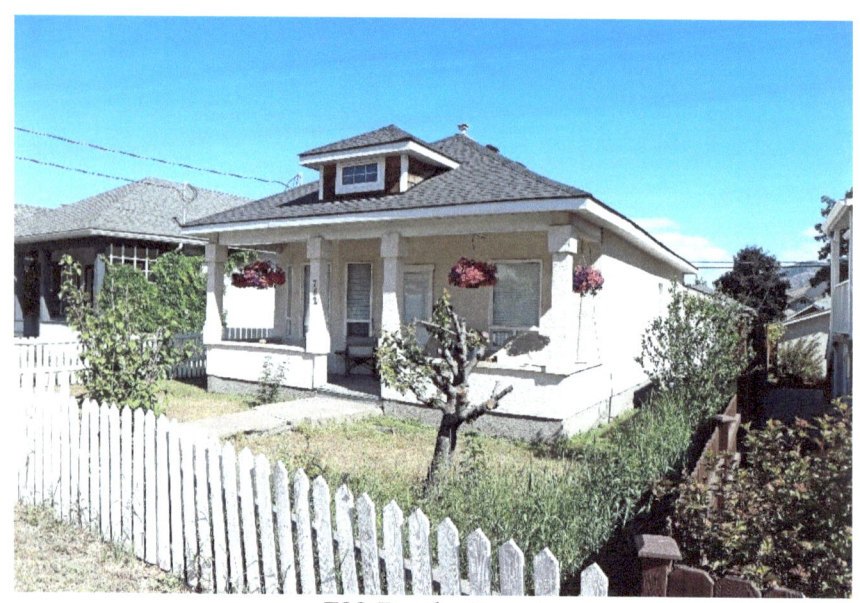

782 Battle Street

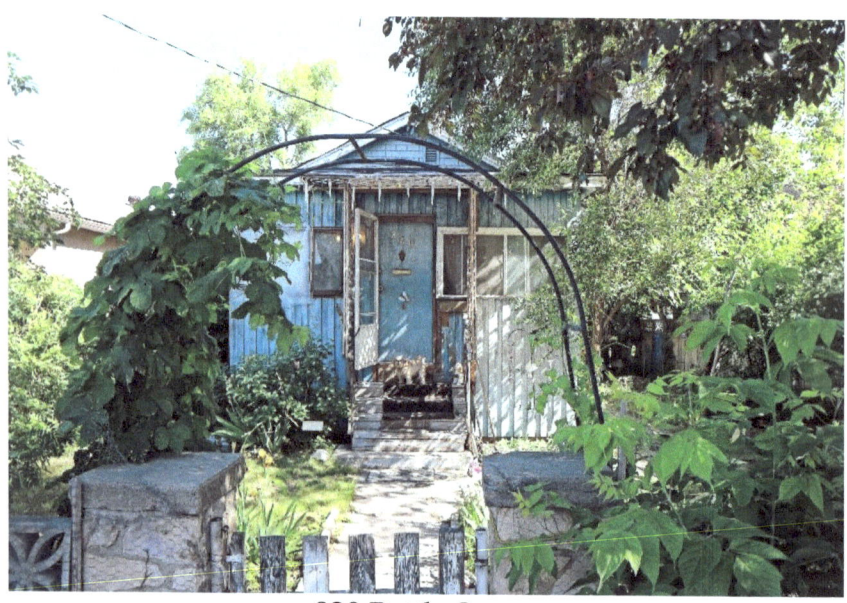

820 Battle Street

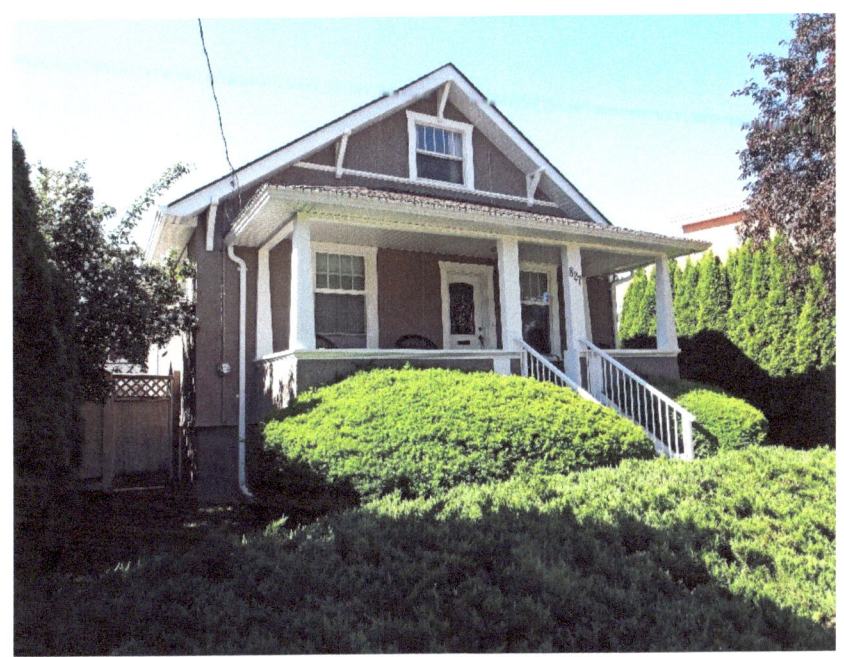

827 Battle Street

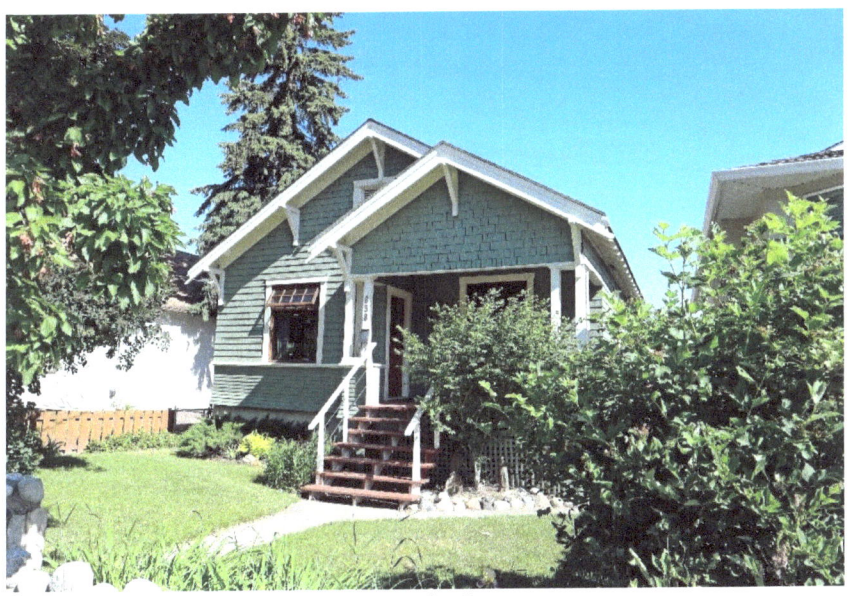

838 Battle Street

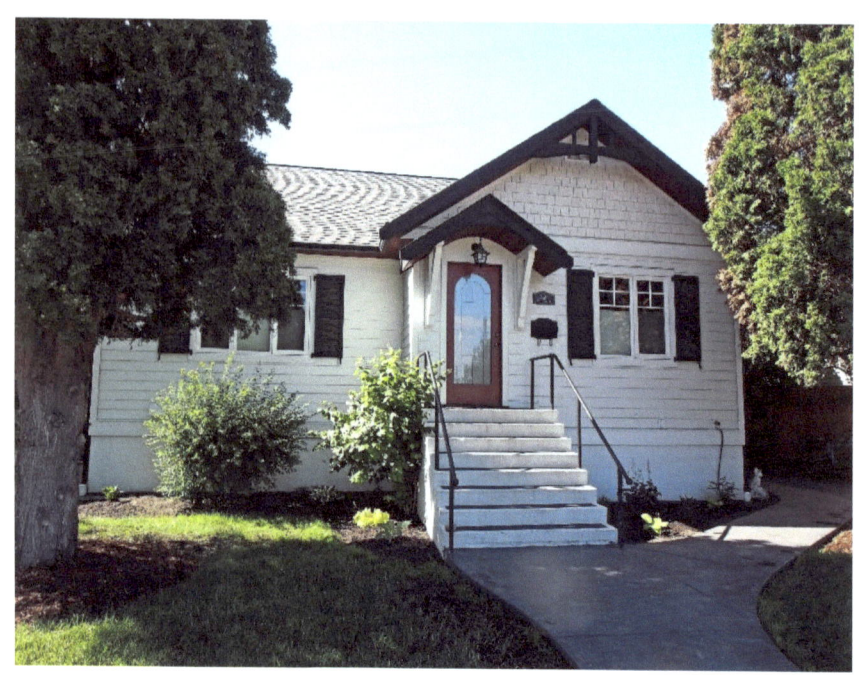

859 Battle Street

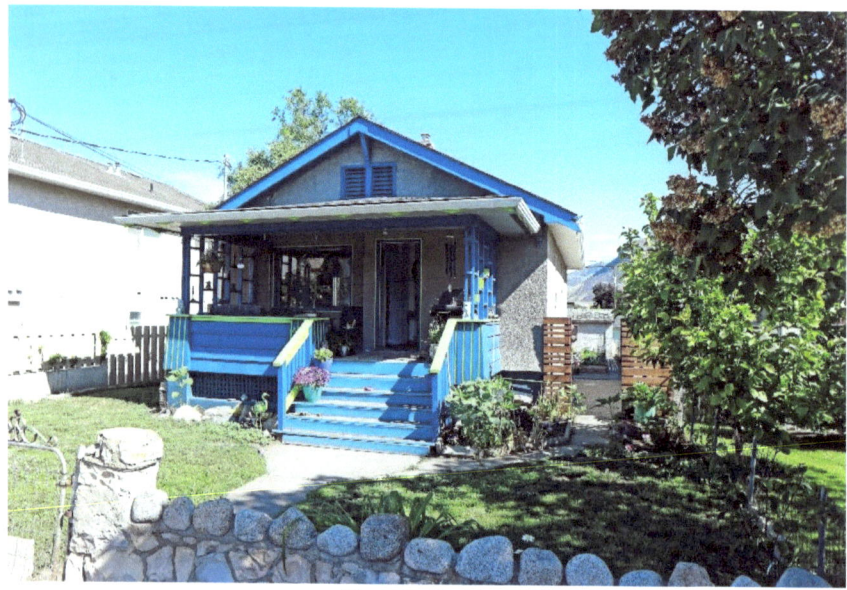

Battle Street

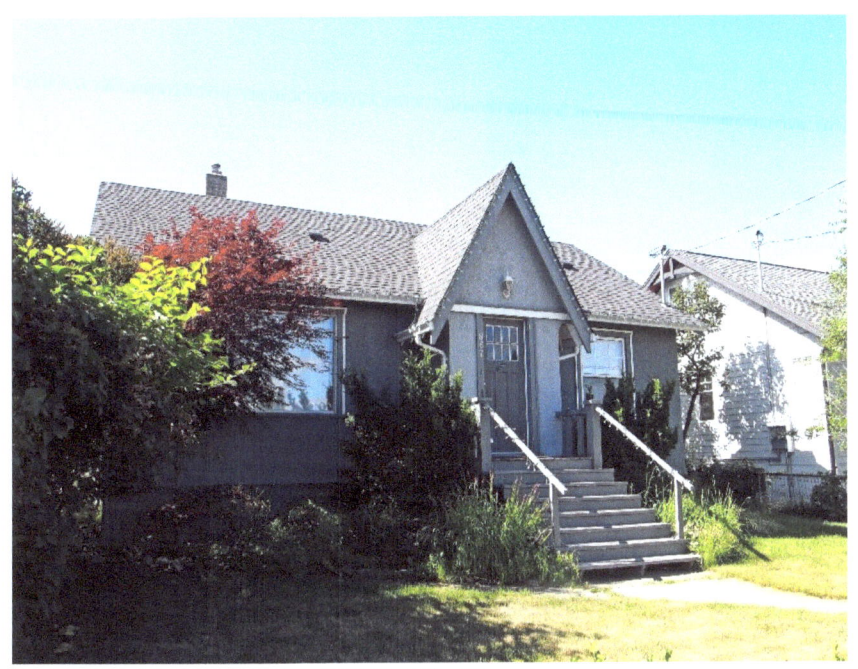

867 Battle Street

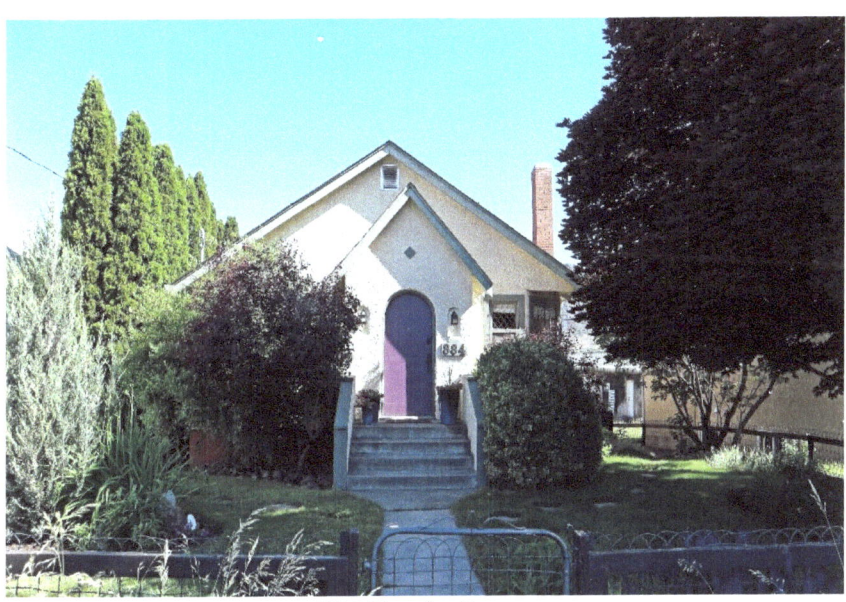

884 Battle Street

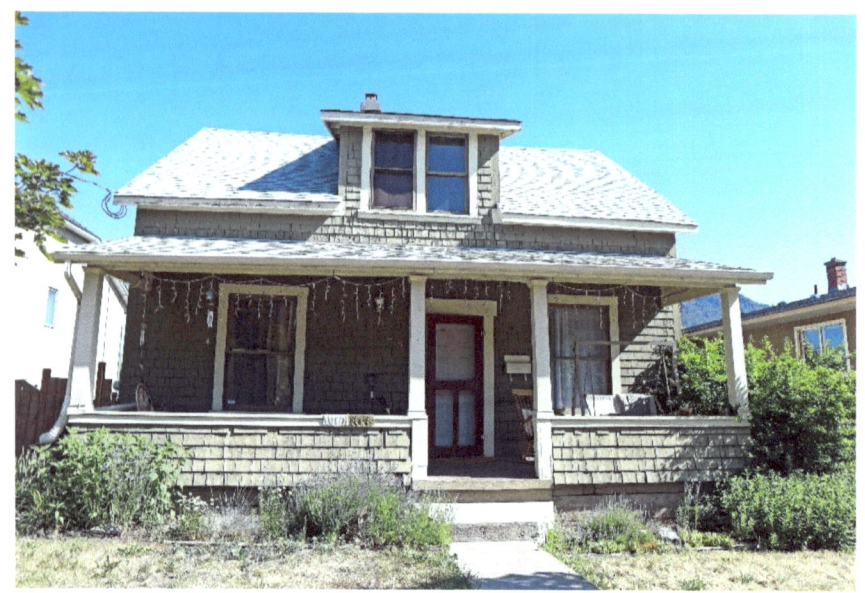
928 Battle Street

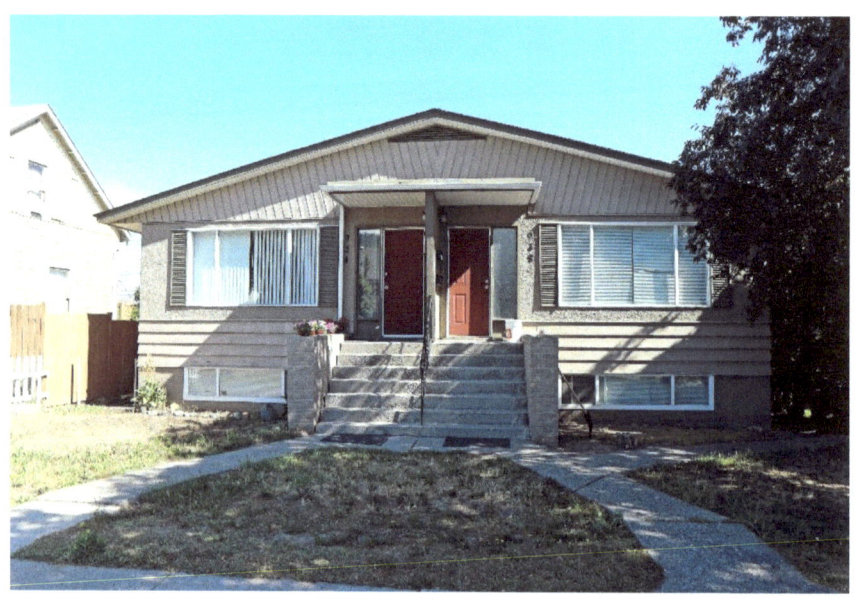
938 Battle Street

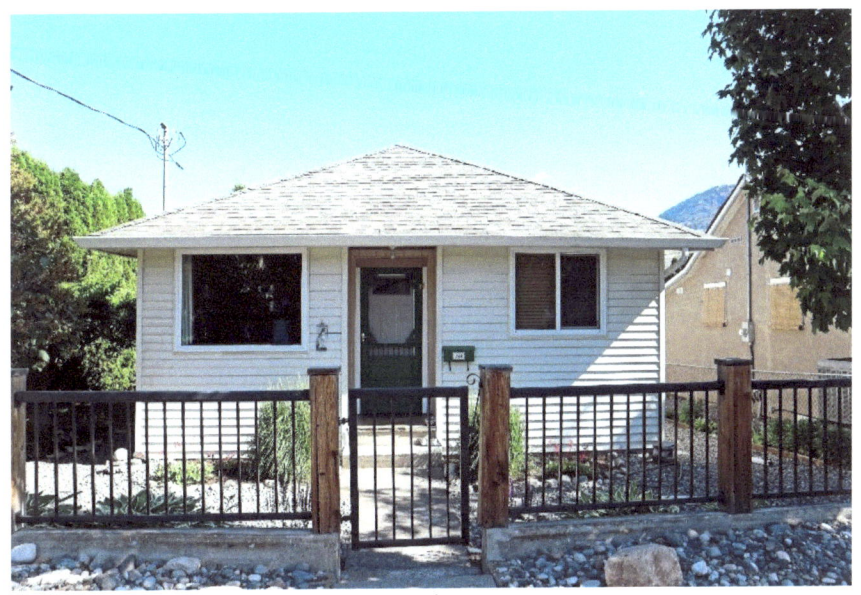

944 Battle Street

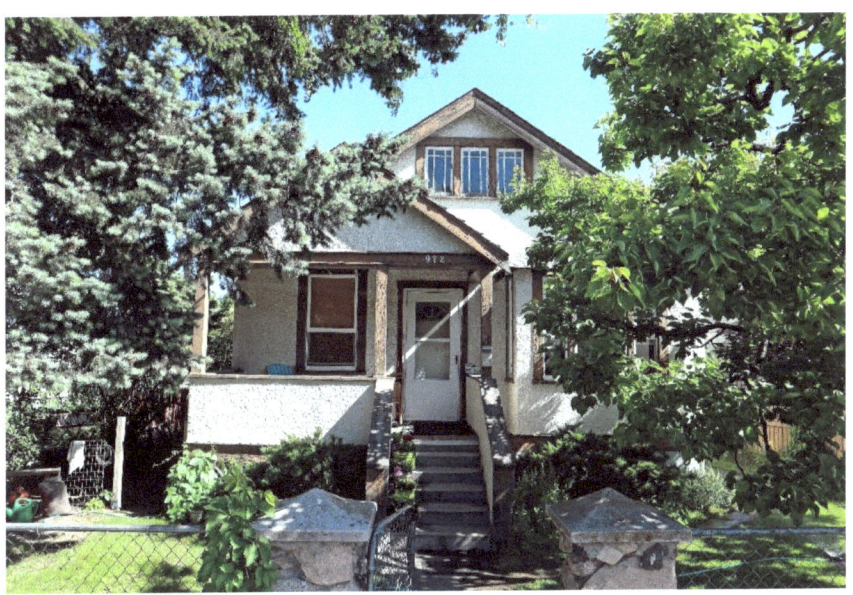

972 Battle Street

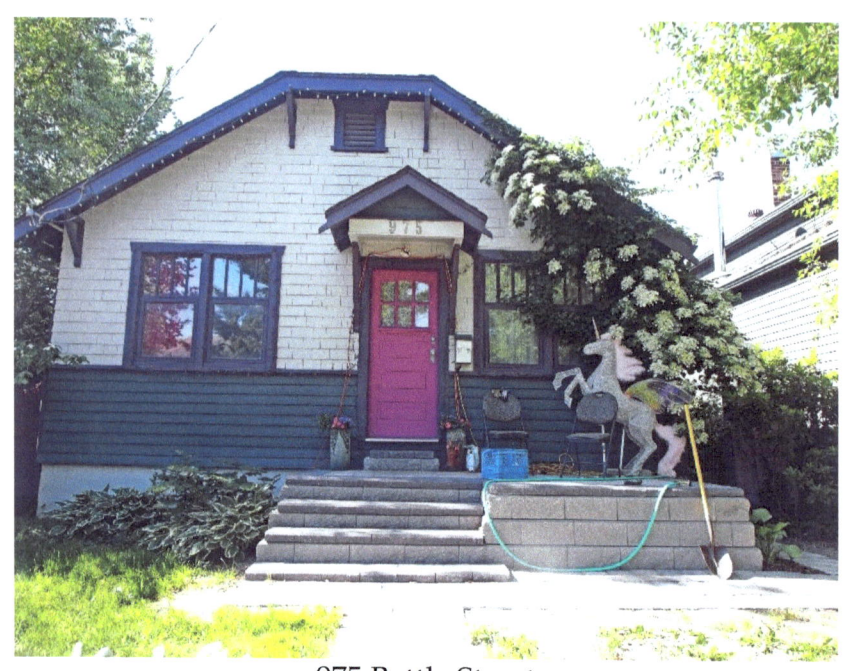
975 Battle Street

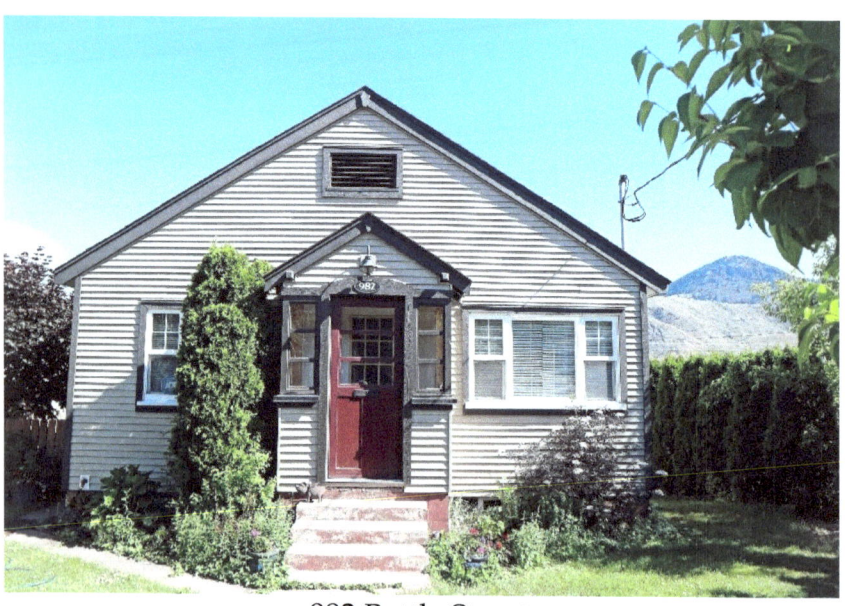
982 Battle Street

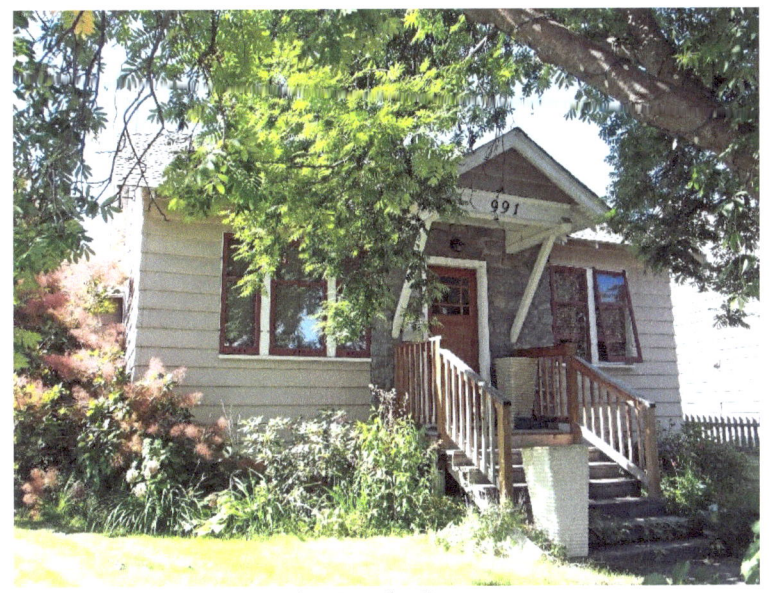

991 Battle Street

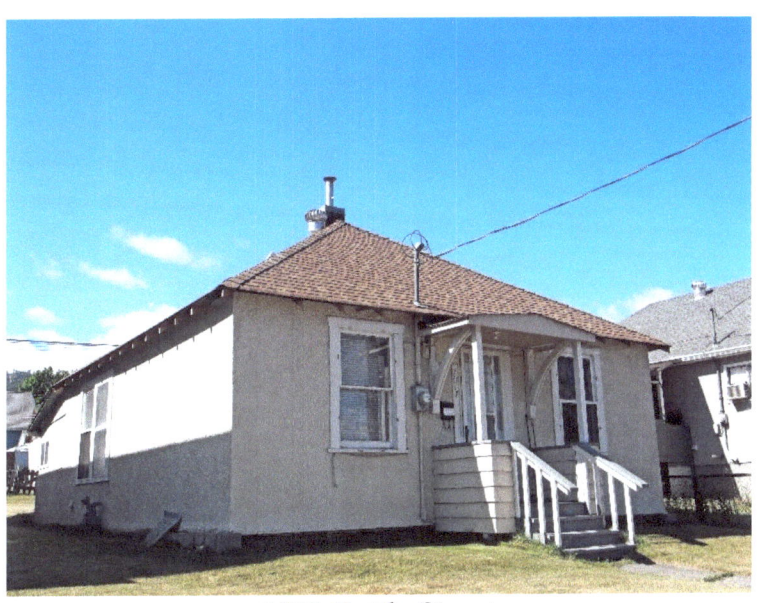

1011 Battle Street

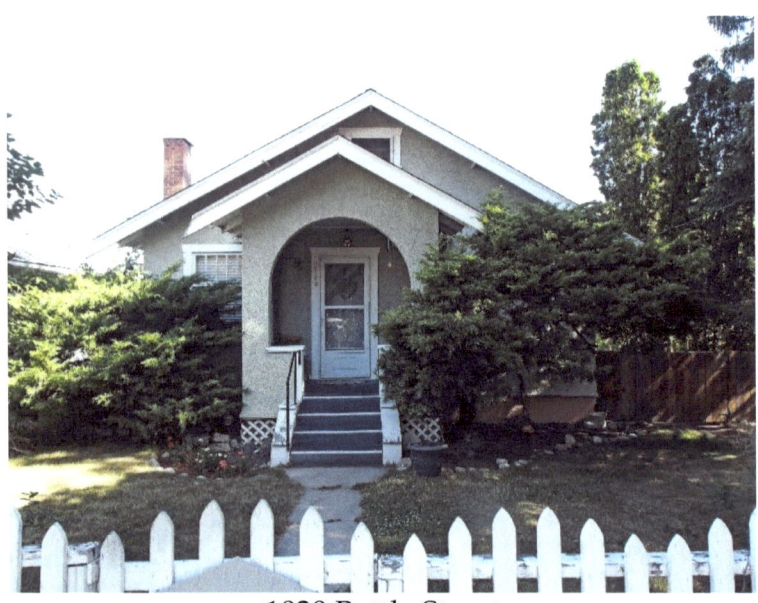

1020 Battle Street

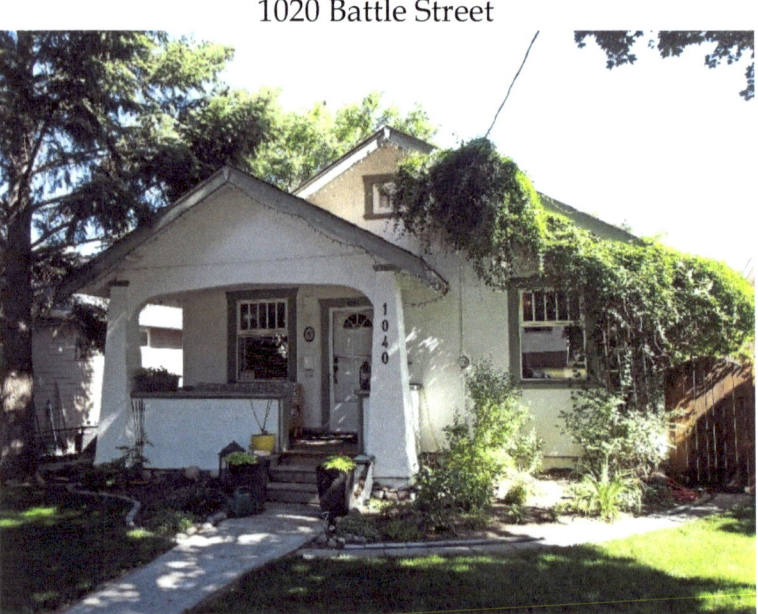

1040 Battle Street - Built in 1930, this Bungalow has original features such as the rough plaster exterior, wood soffits and fascia with some original windows.

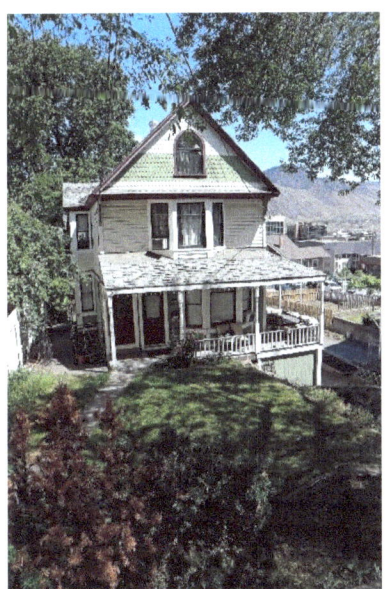

32 Battle Street West

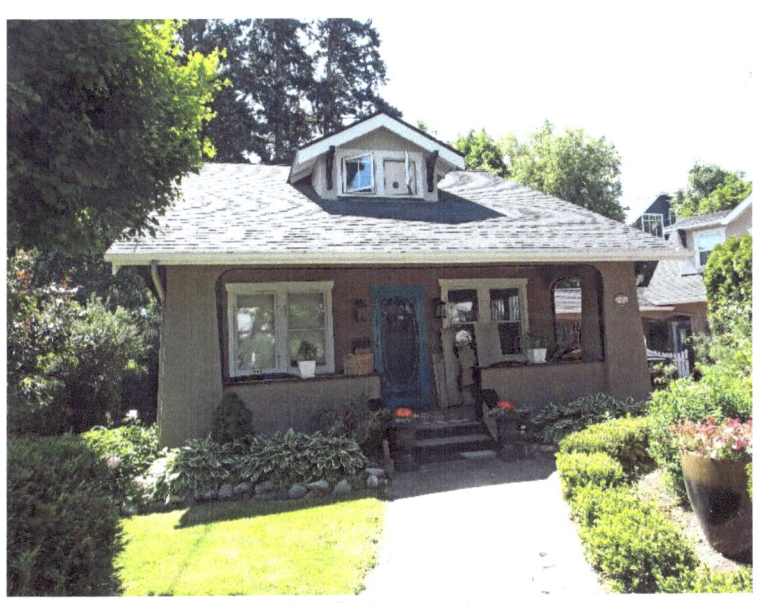

45 Battle Street West

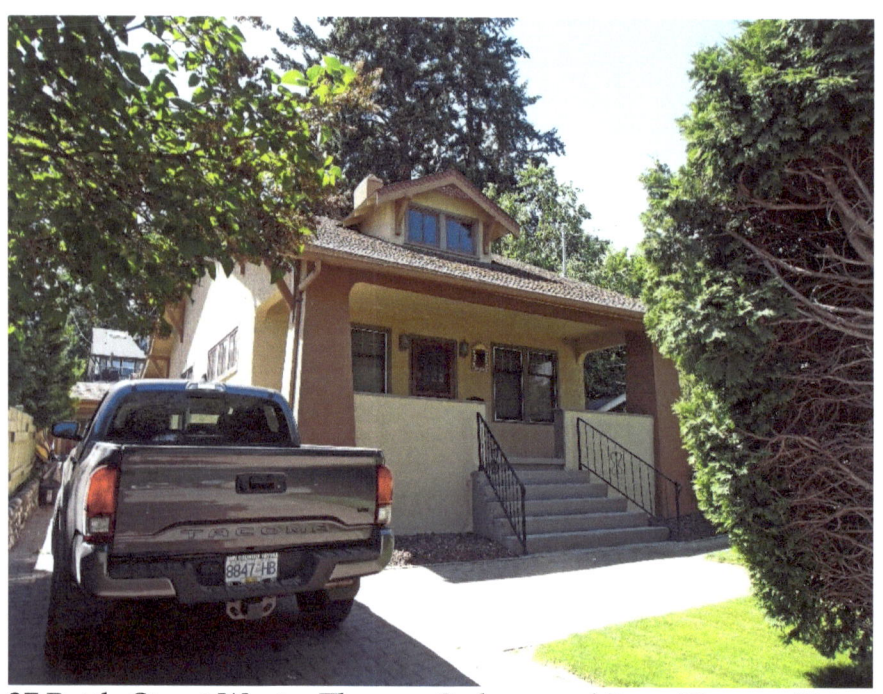

37 Battle Street West – Thomas Sedgewood Ross House - This Cottage style house built in 1926 has plaster siding, multi-pane windows, decorative fascia, and a verandah with two large square pillars at each end.

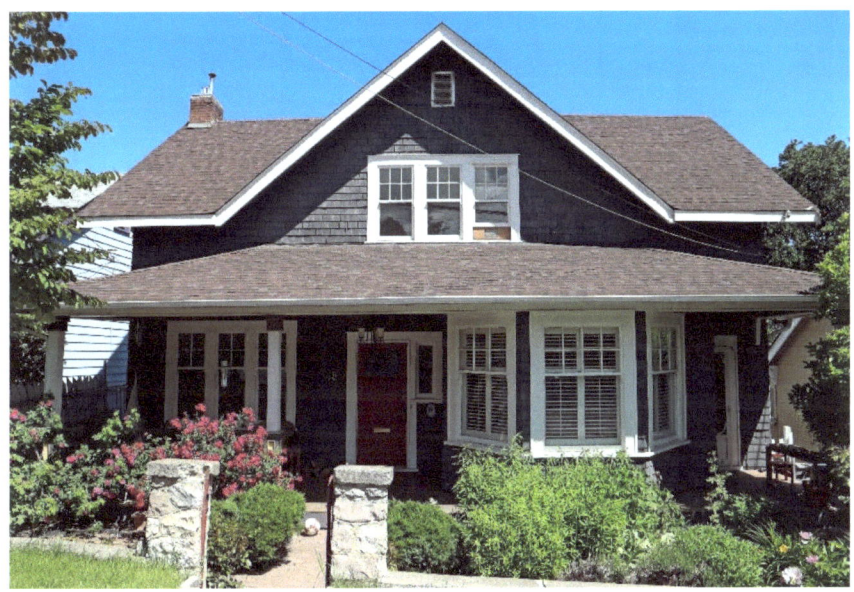

48 Battle Street West – a Roy Burris House - Roy Burris was a member of the famous Kamloops medical family. He had this house built in 1911. It is very similar in style and age to 179 Battle Street West and shares many of the same architectural features. Its long, low verandah is typical of the bungalow style developed by the British in India to keep out the hot, piercing rays of the sun. The verandah boasts the square columns with decorative trim and bay windows typical of the era.

The original cedar shingle siding on this house was spared the unfortunate 'modernizing' stucco facelift that so many houses in the neighborhood fell victim to in the 1940s and 1950s. Cedar siding is a distinguishing characteristic of early Kamloops houses. The windows still have their original glass panes.

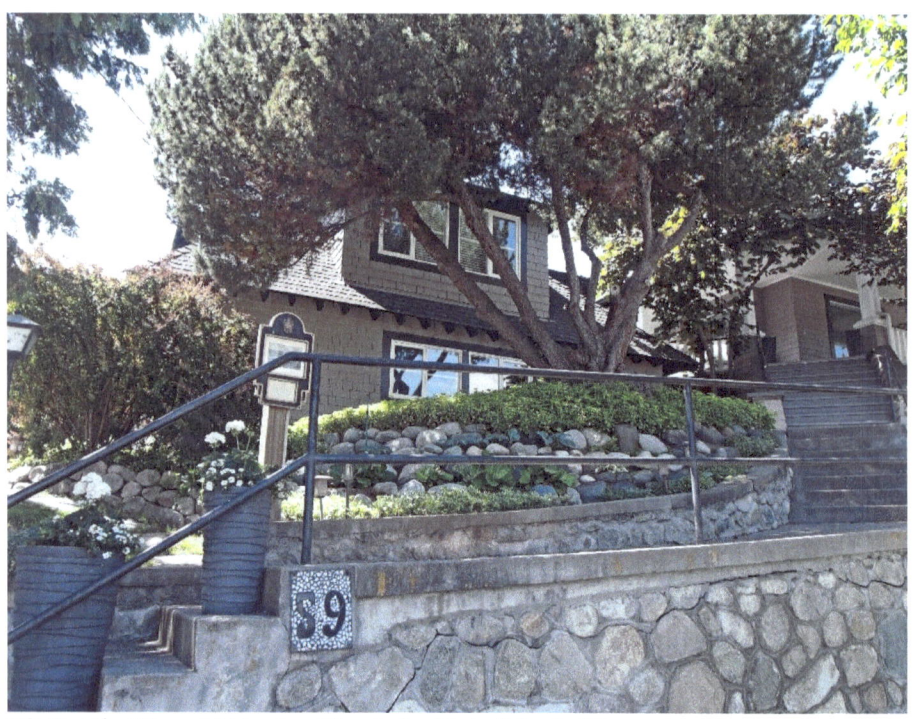

59 Battle Street West – Captain E.A. Nash House – Captain Nash came to Kamloops in the 1890s after serving in the North-West Rebellion of 1885. His beautiful house was built in 1910 along the edge of a deep gully. The style of the house suits a military man. It is a colonial bungalow with a long, low verandah similar to the type built by British officers in India. In Kamloops, the house was built of wood with cedar shingle siding.

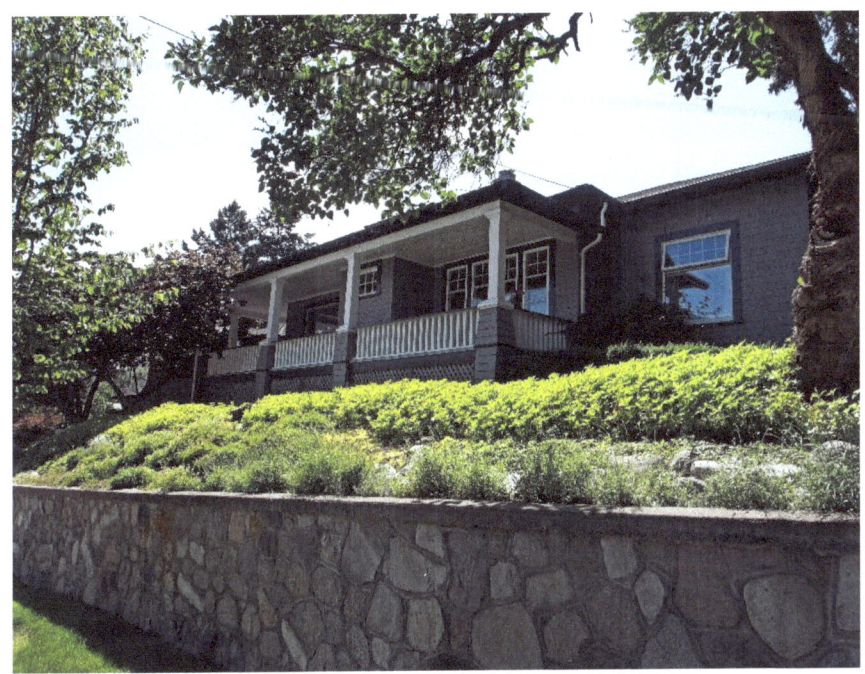

59 Battle Street West

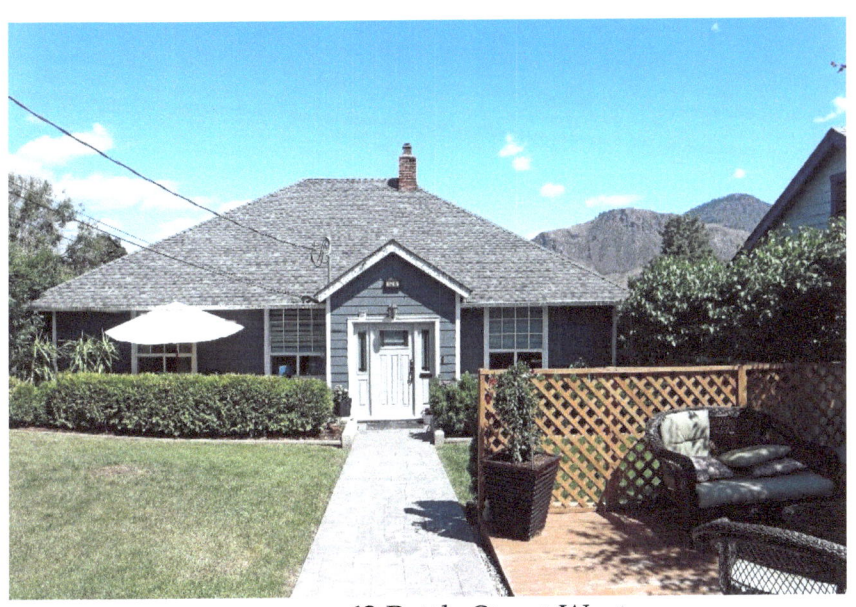

62 Battle Street West

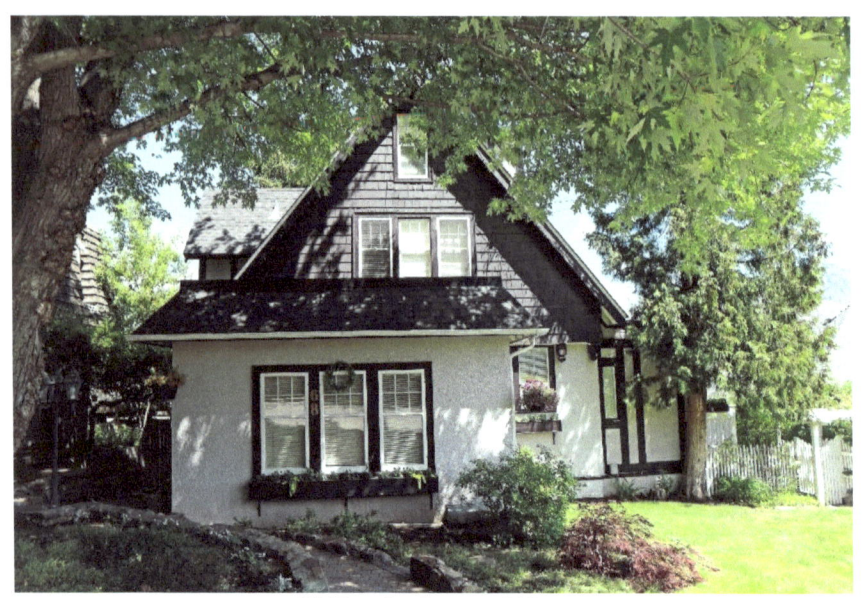

68 Battle Street West

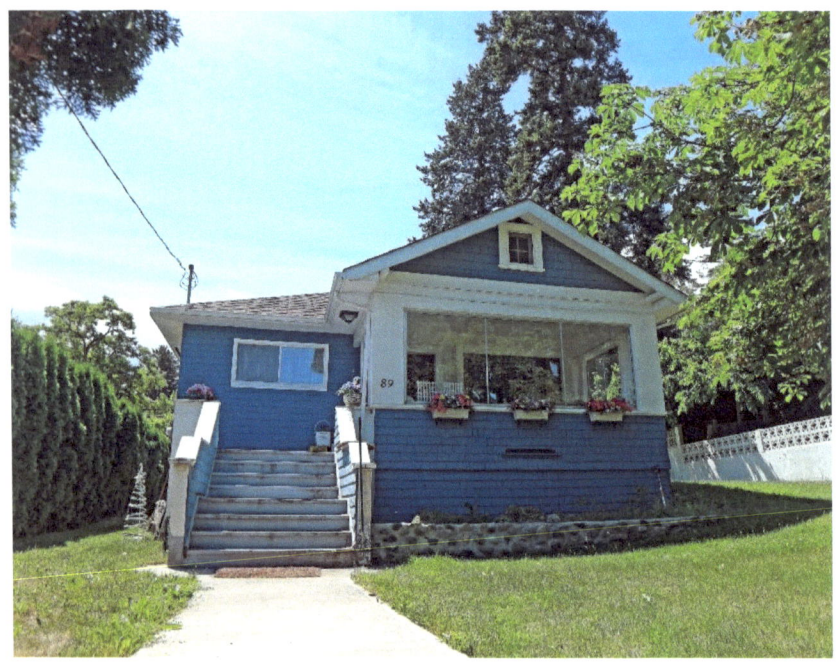

89 Battle Street West

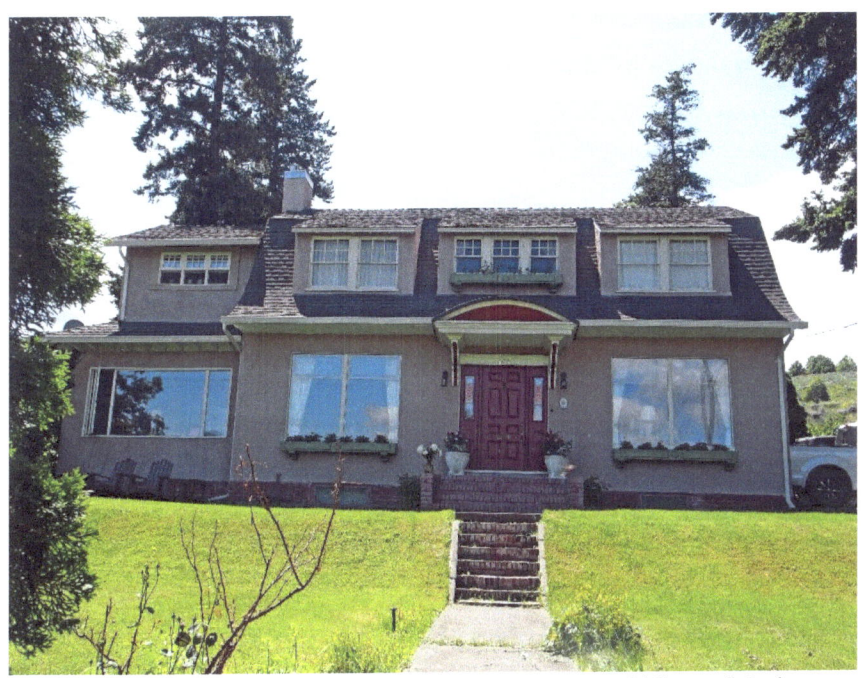

101 Battle Street West – A. Galloway House - When this house was built in 1928, it was considered ultramodern and very forward looking. The red mansard roof, red brick steps, plate glass windows, dormers, window boxes and small front porch with a "Greek porch" roof are all original features. Archibald Galloway owned a pharmacy in Kamloops for many years. He also successfully ran as a City Councilor and was director of many community organizations.

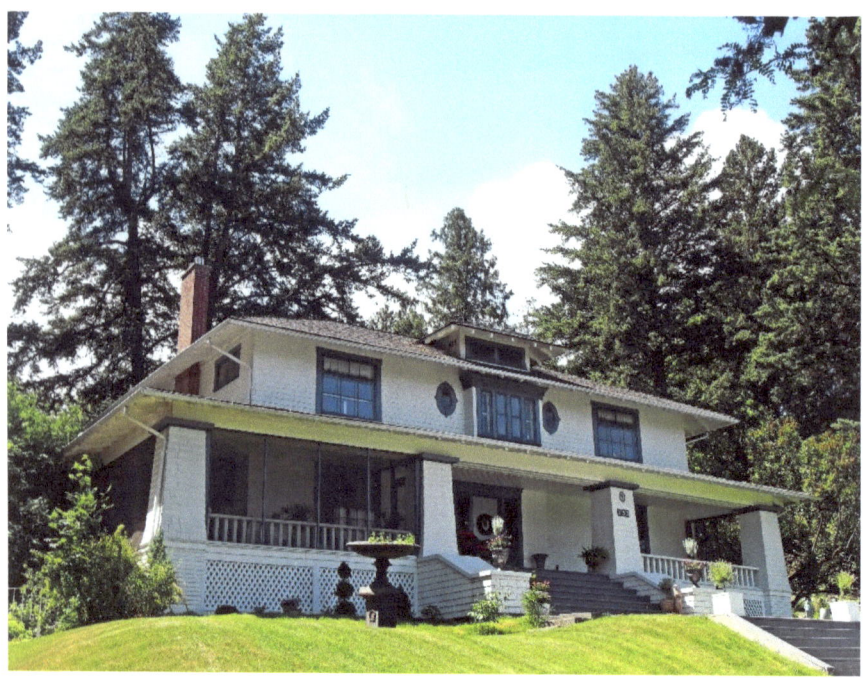

133 Battle Street West – Frederick E. Young House - When this house was built in 1910, it was surrounded by sweeping property which stretched south and east for several lots. The owner, Frederick Young, was owner and publisher of the Kamloops Standard newspaper. A tennis court, croquet area, gazebo, and a stable located at 76 Nicola Street West were part of the property.

The two-storey house has an expansive wraparound verandah accessed by a broad flight of stairs, wide leaded glass windows, two circular windows above the front door, sturdy tapered columns, Craftsman style millwork, exposed rafter ends, and an attic dormer.

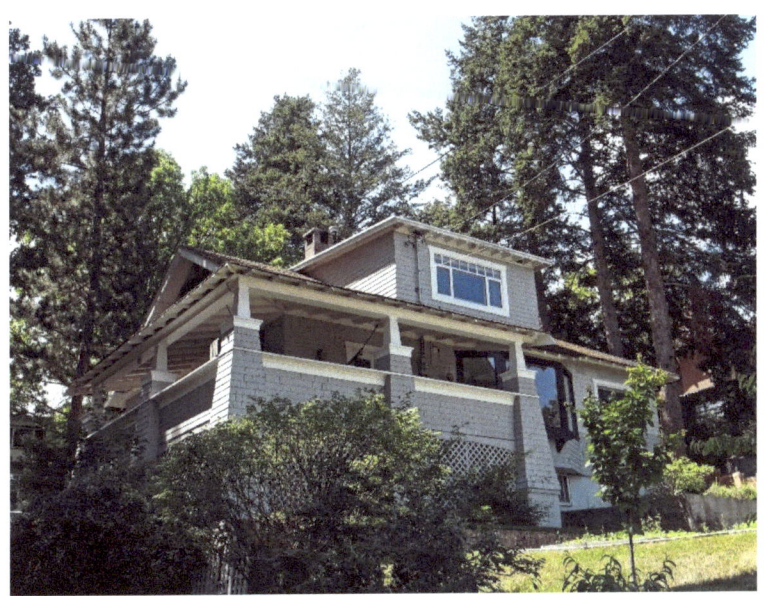

137 Battle Street West

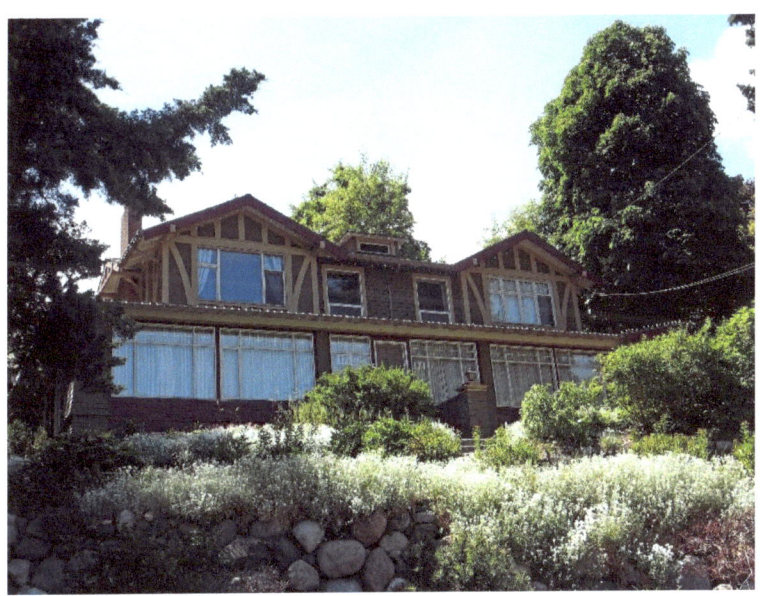

171 Battle Street West

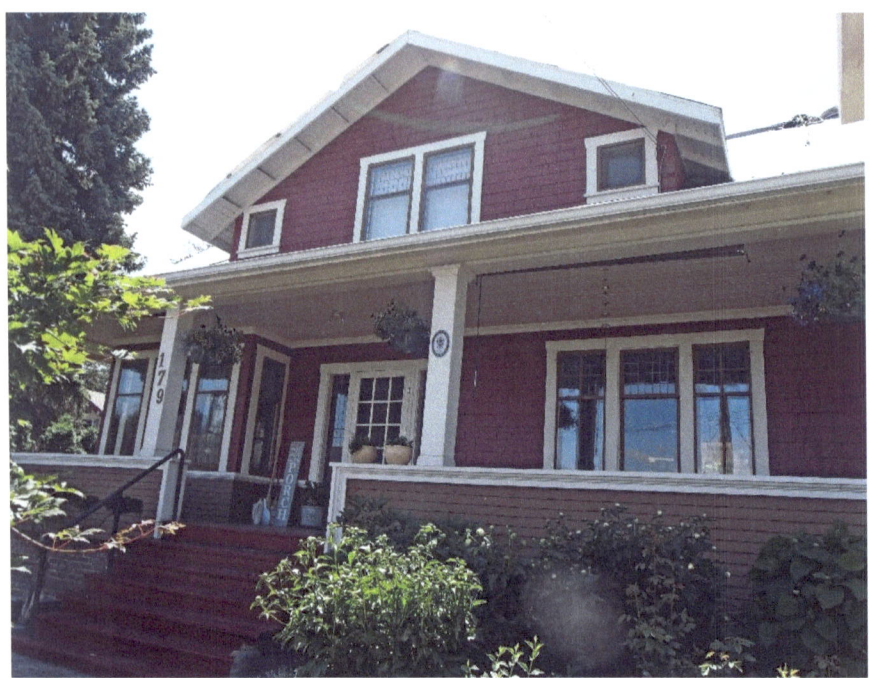

179 Battle Street West – Basil C. Parker House – This house is similar in style to 48 Battle Street West. It has the same long low verandah with square columns that was developed by the British in India to provide a cool sitting area. It retains its original cedar single siding, multi-pane windows and clapboard siding on verandah.

Other Books by Barbara Raue

Coins of Gold
Arrows, Indians and Love
The Life and Times of Barbara
The Cromwell Family Book
Laura Secord Discovered
Daddy Where Are You?

Montana Series
Book 1: Montana Dream
Book 2: Life on the Montana Frontier
Book 3: Montana to Boston and Back
Book 4: Montana Sons Go to War
Book 5: Montana Sons Return from War

Book 1: Rite of Passage
Book 2: Rite of Marriage

© 2019 by Barbara Raue - All the photos in this book have been taken with my cameras. I own the rights to them.

Series Name: Cruising Ontario, Saving Our History One Photo at a Time in colour photos

Books Available in Alphabetical Order:

Aberfoyle, Acton, Ajax, Alton, Amherstburg, Ancaster, Arthur, Auburn, Aylmer, Ayr, Beaver Valley, Belfountain, Belgrave, Belleville, Bloomingdale, Blyth, Brantford, Brockville, Burford, Burgessville, Burlington, Caledon, Caledonia, Cambridge, Carlow, Cayuga, Chatsworth, Cheltenham, Clifford, Colborne, Collingwood, Conestogo, Delhi, Dorchester to Aylmer, Drayton, Drumbo, Dundas, Dunlop, Dunnville, Eden Mills, Elmira, Elora, Embro, Erin, Essex, Fergus, Fort Erie, Georgetown, Goderich, Grimsby, Guelph, Hagersville, Haldimand County, Hamilton, Hanover, Harriston, Hespeler, Ingersoll, Inglewood, Innerkip, Jarvis, Kingston, Kingsville, Kitchener, Lake Superior, Lincoln, Linwood, Listowel, London, Lucknow, Merrickville, Mono, Mount Brydges, Mount Forest, Mount Pleasant, Neustadt, New Hamburg, Newboro, Newport, Niagara-on-the-Lake, Niagara Falls, North Bay, Norwich, Oakville, Onondaga, Orangeville, Orillia, Oshawa, Otterville, Owen Sound, Palmerston, Paris, Parry Sound, Pelham, Perth, Peterborough, Petrolia, Pickering, Port Colborne, Port Elgin, Port Hope, Port Perry, Portland, Preston, Rockwood, Sarnia, Sault Ste. Marie, Seaforth, Sheffield, Shelburne, Simcoe, Smiths Falls, Smithville, Southampton, Southwest Oxford, St. Catharines, St. George, St. Jacobs, St. Marys, St. Thomas, Stoney Creek, Stouffville, Stratford, Strathroy, Sudbury, Tavistock, Terra Cotta, Thamesford, Thunder Bay, Tillsonburg, Toronto, Uxbridge, Waterdown, Waterford, Waterloo, Welland, Wellesley, West Flamborough, Westport, Whitby, Windsor, Wingham, Woodstock, York, Zorra

Book 237: Tavistock, Innerkip
Book 238-239: Ingersoll
Book 240: Zorra Township
Book 241: Southwest Oxford
Book 242: Otterville, Burgessville
Book 243: Norwich
Book 244: Woodstock Book 4

www.ingramcontent.com/pod-product-compliance
Lightning Source LLC
Chambersburg PA
CBHW040226220526
45473CB00001B/142